DOWN-TO-EARTH

GARDENING

KNOW-HOW FOR THE '90s

DOWN-TO-EARTH
GARDENING
KNOW-HOW FOR THE '90s

Vegetables & Herbs

DICK RAYMOND

A Storey Publishing Book

Storey Communications, Inc.
Pownal, Vermont 05261

Cover design and art by Carol Jessop
Text design by Cindy McFarland
Cover photograph by Paul Boisvert
Text photos by Paul Boisvert and Dick Raymond
Edited by Dave Schaefer and Ben Watson
Illustrations by Mike Belanger, Barbara Carter, Charles Cook, Judy Eliason, Brigita Fuhrmann,
Charles Joslin, Alison Kolesar, Michael Lamb, Carol MacDonald,
and David Sylvester

Some of the material in this book was originally published in
Down-to-Earth Vegetable Gardening Know-How by Dick Raymond (Garden Way Publishing, 1975).

Down-To-Earth Gardening Know-How for the 90s

Printed in the United States by Courier
Sixth Printing, May 1994

Library of Congress Cataloging-in-Publication Data

Raymond, Dick.
    Down to earth gardening know-how for the '90s : vegetables & herbs
/Dick Raymond. — 3rd ed.
        p. cm.
    "A Storey Publishing book."
    Includes index.
    ISBN 0-88266-649-5 (pbk.)
    1. Vegetable gardening. 2. Herb gardening. I. Title.
SB321.R327 1991
635—dc20   90-50416
                                                              CIP

CONTENTS

BACK
TO THE GARDEN FOR THE 1990'S

WHEN THE FIRST EDITION of this book came out nearly 20 years ago I said in the introduction that anyone can garden successfully. All you need is access to a small piece of land, a few simple tools, a minimum of knowledge, a little spare time, and some ambition.

Those facts are still true today.

But how much has changed since then, too!

All the changes were going through my mind when I sat down and reread the original *Down-to-Earth*. After 20 printings, the publisher, John Storey, wanted me to undertake the first complete revision of the book.

Times have changed, all right. All you have to do to see the changes is pick up today's newspaper.

You'll see that a lot more women have entered the workplace. With both people in many households off making a living, I want to share all the new fast and easy methods I have learned in the last 20 years, to make your

"Shop in your own produce department first" is a good idea to remember for gardeners who want to get the most from their gardens. Check your garden, your freezer, and your root cellar. Make a list and plan your meals before you go to the supermarket. Even small lots and condos have space for a well-planned garden.

Once you've tasted one of your own tomatoes fresh off the vine and warmed by the sun, you'll want to have a garden every year. The home gardener can keep pesticides, herbicides, and fungicides off the vegetables he or she grows.

You can store, freeze, and preserve vegetables to last until the next growing season if you decide to scale up to a "harvest garden." Jan and I have had a root cellar in good times and bad for most of our lives.

garden more productive with less work and in less time.

People today are often short of both time and space but still want a fresh, bountiful harvest. So I've added a lot of new ideas and tips about gardening in small spaces, containers, and less-than-perfect conditions. Many beginners don't realize that they can mix flowers and vegetables and herbs to have both fresh food for the table and a beautiful display in the same space.

Above all, health and environmental issues have changed the way we all live. The widespread use of herbicides and pesticides has raised serious questions about what is in what we eat. We now know that pesticides banned in this country come back in produce grown outside our borders. Just about the only way to be sure of what's in your food is to grow it yourself. This book was updated to include what I have learned about gardening with the blessing of Mother Nature, not fighting her all the time.

Gardeners have always been environmental activists . . . probably without realizing it. The good gardener recycles throwaway materials, composts organic wastes, and rebuilds the soil. He or she may never carry placards in an environmental protest, but year after year these gardeners leave their little piece of the earth better than they found it. Richer, more productive, less wasteful. Now, as many cities make it illegal to send yard wastes to overcrowded landfills, the gardener just shrugs and asks, "What's new?" Gardeners have been turning this material into compost or mulch all along! It's impossible to be a good gardener without living in harmony with nature. For those of us who grew up in the country this was not a matter of environmental concern, it was just good "horse sense."

Kids take to gardens like ducks to water if you give them a little patch of their own. What better thing to teach a youngster than how to take care of the earth and grow their own food? My wife, Jan, spends a lot of time in the garden with our grandchildren.

The truth of the matter is that people are gardeners because they just plain love to do it. Only a gardener knows the real taste of a tomato picked from the garden at the peak of ripeness and sliced into a salad moments later. Or fresh fish grilled on the barbecue with a sprig of your own fresh tarragon. Soon you begin to realize that there are many varieties of vegetables you have never tasted before, and each is very different and unique. Gardeners compare notes on varieties the way wine experts compare notes. I have updated the sections on varieties to include 20 more years of experience to make sure you get off to a good start.

The act of gardening is a pleasure in itself. While we cannot create life, we can create the conditions that allow it to develop and flourish. Seeing a garden blossom is a little like watching our children grow up. Patience. Encouragement. Protection. Knowledge. Care. These are what it takes to be a good gardener.

In the process, the gardener can turn an average home into a place of real beauty and productivity. Personally, I think mowing lawns is as boring an activity as a human being can undertake. But gardening is one of the most rewarding. Many gardeners, myself included, walk out to the garden just to look at and enjoy it. Just to see what changes have taken place since our last visit less than a day ago. Around the world, gardens are important for the mind as well as for the body. Maybe that time is coming to the United States.

In revising *Down-to-Earth* I tried to leave it as the basic book for beginners that it was intended to be. I have added some fun activities for children, because gardening should be a family activity. Nothing does a better job of teaching youngsters how to take care of the earth that is the source of all we have. I also think the experienced gardener will find this a very useful book. Many of the charts took years to develop and can't be found anywhere else. I often think of a comment from a person who has become a well-known gardener himself: "This was the book that taught me to garden. Today, if I had to get rid of an entire library of gardening books and keep just one, this would be the one I'd keep."

To me, it will be a success if sharing more than 40 years of gardening know-how will help make gardening for you as much of a joy as it has been for me and my family.

Happy Gardening,
Dick Raymond
March 1991

CHAPTER 1
PLANNING
YOUR DREAM GARDEN

THE FIRST STEP in planning your garden is to decide what you expect from it. Gardens come in as many sizes and shapes as you can imagine. Generally, though, there are four types of gardens: Salad or mini-gardens, summer gardens, winter storage gardens, and "have-more" or cash crop gardens.

Salad or Mini-Gardens

Salad gardens are very small. They might be in a container, like half a whiskey barrel, or just a strip of vegetables, flowers, and herbs along the edge of your patio. The best place for a salad garden is near the house. A sunny spot just outside the kitchen door might be a perfect place. Just one step out the door and you can find fresh herbs, a little lettuce, tomatoes, onions, radishes, peppers . . . all the makings for a fresh salad every day. You can even mix enough vegetables for a salad garden right in amongst your flower beds. Flowers and vegetables make good and beautiful neighbors. For example, a border of salad greens with taller flowers in the background makes an attractive and productive garden.

Summer Gardens

The summer garden is one that keeps a family eating fresh produce during the growing season, and provides a little surplus to freeze or preserve some peas, tomatoes, peppers, broccoli, and cauliflower. Or you can share with a neighbor who doesn't have a garden. Summer gardens can provide you with a continuous supply of many kinds of vegetables grown in succession throughout the season.

Winter Storage Gardens

The winter storage garden provides enough for the family to eat during the summer as well as enough to freeze, dry, can, or store for the winter. It is a combination of the summer garden vegetables and other crops like corn, potatoes, and winter squash that occupy more space. By freezing and storing vegetables, this

Deep winter is "dream time". . . a good time to start planning your garden. A lot of valuable information is available in mail-order seed catalogs, so be sure to write away for catalogs before you start planning.

kind of garden lets you enjoy your harvested produce all winter long.

The "Have-More" Garden

The "have-more" garden is planned so that you grow more than you want to consume, and you sell the surplus as a home business. It can really pay for one person to spend extra time in the garden. For example, with just 10,000 square feet, plus some marketing know-how, you can grow $4,000 to $7,000 worth of vegetables. You get to keep most of what you earn, and the equipment you need (if any) is tax-deductible. If this means that you can avoid buying a second car just to get to work, the benefits really start adding up. Tending a have-more garden at home may also allow one person in the family to spend a lot more time with young children, saving the price of a babysitter or day-care center. You can also save on clothing, gasoline, and other costs associated with hav-

ing a "normal" job. If you love to garden and have the necessary growing space, you can almost certainly find a local market for organically grown vegetables.

At our home, all garden planning starts right after New Year's Day when the seed catalogs start arriving. Get several seed catalogs, even if you don't plan to buy from all of them. These catalogs contain wonderful information about each vegetable and, often, color photographs that can help your planning. For example, you'll learn about how different varieties of the same vegetable compare with each other, how many days each variety needs from planting to harvest (this will help you plan for succession crops), and about varieties that have special disease resistance. The pictures will give you an idea of how large the plants grow to be and how much space they'll need.

Most good seed catalogs also have a zone map that will tell you which growing zone you live in, and what vegetables will grow in that zone. Your growing zone is based on the date of the last frost in the spring and the first frost in the fall, as well as other climatic information.

To find out the average frost dates for your region, see the maps on page 10. Seed catalogs, your county Extension Service, or the local TV weatherman will be able to give you more exact dates. Write this information down wherever you keep your garden plan, because you'll use these dates every year.

Some Garden Planning Tips

❦ Whichever garden type you choose, start by sketching out exactly where you are going to put each vegetable and herb.

❦ Many garden plans are based on where the sun is coming from . . . the south. Short plants are at the front of the garden—the south end—and the tall ones are at the back—the north end. This prevents tall plants from shading shorter ones. Just imagine a staircase of plants that begins with lettuce on the south end and climbs to corn or sunflowers on the north. In northern states this provides full sun. In southern states you may want to reverse the order to provide cool shade during hot weather. Seed catalogs will tell you how high the plants grow, and this helps you plan. Flower gardeners do the same thing to create a beautiful display. Or mix flowers and vegetables up the staircase to create both good eating and a beautiful display. Remember, some plants like a little shade during the hot days of summer—lettuce, for example — and you can plan a second crop for a shady spot.

🐛 Be careful about the varieties you select for a summer garden. Don't choose more than two or three varieties of each vegetable. Choose the ones that do well in your area. As you get more experienced you can experiment with different varieties. You'll find favorites of your own, but try the old standbys first. Check the "sure crop recommendations" in the Garden Planning Chart on pages 176-183 to see which varieties I suggest. Ask a neighbor who gardens to help you choose the varieties that grow best where you are. Your local garden center can help out, too.

🐛 Try to decide just how much of each vegetable you will need, and allow

You can cut your garden space in half if you use wide rows like this one. Wide rows can be 16 or 20 inches wide—the width of your garden rake—or even double that. Peas and beans can be planted in blocks 6 feet wide or more.

enough space on your plan. A 25' x 30' plot is just about the right size for a summer garden to feed a family of four.

🐛 For the most productive garden, plan to use wide rows. Now is a good time to read ahead in the section on wide-row planting (see Chapter 6) to figure out how much to plant. As a rule of thumb, you will need three times as many seeds to plant the same length of row, but you'll get three times the harvest, so you can cut back on the size of your garden. Your wide row only needs to

You can harvest two, three, and in some areas four crops a season by following early crops with later ones. Here, I'm turning under lettuce to be followed by a crop of beans. This is called *succession planting*. See the chart on page 9 for helpful ideas.

be one-quarter to one-third as long as a single row, depending on the variety of vegetable.

☙ It is possible to get two crops, one after the other, in the same space during one growing season. This is called *succession planting*. For example, peas planted early in the spring will be done by midsummer, and can be followed by carrots or broccoli and other crops for a fall harvest. See the chart on page 9 for suggestions on which crops can follow others in succession.

☙ If you're planning a mini-garden or container garden, look for small-space varieties of tomatoes, squash, and cucumbers. These produce normal-sized vegetables on smaller plants. For tomatoes, Patio and Pixie are good choices. I've tried so-called "miniature vegetables" and have always been unhappy with the results. They take up three-quarters of the space needed for full-sized vegetables, but when you

harvest there's not enough to eat to make them worthwhile.

☙ Your seed catalog will come in handy all the while as you plan. For example, it will tell you the number of days from planting to harvest for each variety. With your frost dates in mind you can calculate if you can expect a harvest in your area, or if you have time to make a succession planting. If you plan early and can't find the varieties you want at your garden center, you can still send for some. Usually, however, the seed racks in your area will contain seeds for plants that do well there.

☙ If you plan to do succession planting, buy your seeds in the spring for that midseason crop. The seed racks may be empty or even cleared out by the time you're ready for a second planting.

Corn and potatoes in particular take up a lot of garden space, and corn is hard to protect from raccoons and birds. Think twice about corn if you only have a small space.

Some Successful Successions

Some vegetables take up garden space all summer because it takes them that long to ripen. Others mature much faster, and once these have been harvested or have passed their peak, the space they occupied will stand idle unless you make use of it. You are harvesting the summer sun's energy as it becomes a crop of vegetables, so it is wasteful to have a single unproductive spot in your garden. Exposed soil dries out faster than soil covered with a crop, so you may have to water bare areas more. Get something growing there! Planting succession crops is the answer. These are crops that can be planted after a previous fast-maturing crop has been harvested.

Crops that mature early include radishes, beans, peas, beets, cauliflower, cabbage, kohlrabi, onions from sets, mustard, spinach, turnips, and early corn.

As soon as these have been harvested, either pull them up and put the plant residue in the compost pile, or turn them directly back into the garden soil. They will be easier to turn back into the soil if you run over them with a rotary mower set at the highest setting.

Plan to have a succession crop ready to go in. It's not a good idea to plant the same crop that was there before. If there were beans in an area, replace them with carrots or beets. Some crops can be planted more than once in the same growing season, but others don't do well during really hot weather—peas, lettuce, and spinach, for example. I wait until late July or August before replanting these vegetables so that they will mature during the cool days of fall.

As you plan your succession crops, use early-maturing varieties. The later varieties take too long to mature, and there is likely to be a frost before the last plantings have a chance to make it. Also, as days grow short, plants will try to set seeds and may produce a tough, stunted crop if they are not near maturity.

It pays to experiment a little with different types of vegetables and to gamble that the first fall frost will be late rather than early. I usually take this chance. Sometimes I win and

HOME VEGETABLE GARDEN SUCCESSION CROPS

Some Grown Early

beans, bush snap	kohlrabi
beans, pole snap	lettuce, leaf
beets	okra
broccoli	onion sets
cabbage	peas
carrots	peppers
cauliflower	radishes
corn, sweet	spinach
cucumbers	squash, summer
eggplant	tomatoes
kale	turnips

Some Grown Late

beans	kohlrabi
beets	lettuce
broccoli	radishes
cabbage	rutabagas
cauliflower	spinach
endive	turnips
kale	

As soon as the early crop is harvested and removed, the later crop is planted.

Examples: early spinach followed by late spinach; early peas followed by late lettuce, kohlrabi, or snap beans; green onions followed by turnips; snap beans followed by beets, etc.

sometimes I lose. But if frost kills some of my later plantings, I don't feel that I have lost much.

Good Companions

There are many combinations of crops that do well side by side in the same row. Some plants will help each other by shading one another or

AVERAGE FROST DATES

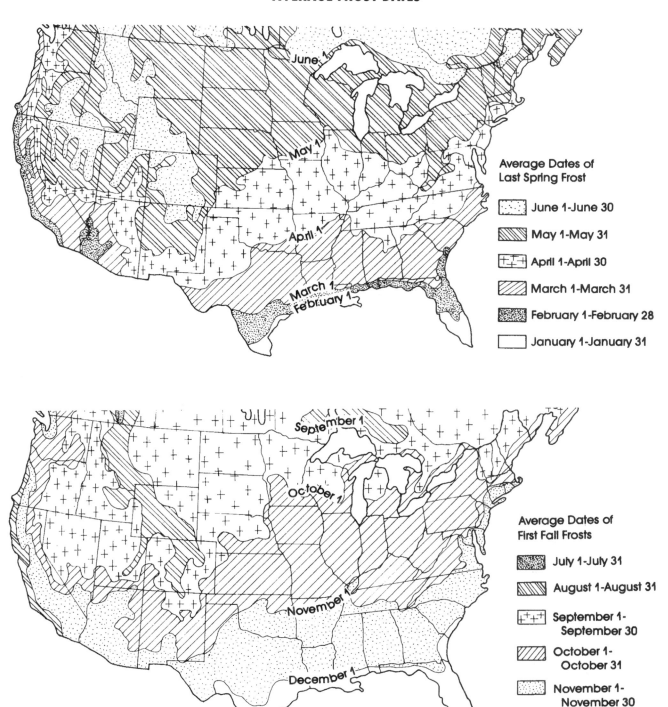

Average Dates of Last Spring Frost

- June 1-June 30
- May 1-May 31
- April 1-April 30
- March 1-March 31
- February 1-February 28
- January 1-January 31

Average Dates of First Fall Frosts

- July 1-July 31
- August 1-August 31
- September 1-September 30
- October 1-October 31
- November 1-November 30
- December 1-December 31

With good advance planning, you won't have to buy a vegetable for your family all summer, even from a garden as small as this 10 x 20 footer. You may even have extra crops to share with friends, neighbors, and shut-ins.

by acting as insect repellents. Beans seem to go well with corn; radishes go with just about anything, and they come up early to mark where your rows are. Parsley does well with both onions and carrots. It is always a good idea to plant something else with parsnips because they take so long to come up. I plant icicle radishes with my parsnips.

If you plant a vegetable that matures before another in the same row, harvest whatever is ripe and allow the other plants to take over the space that has just been vacated. This way, you can get more out of a small space. There are a number of combinations that you can try: radishes with carrots (or almost anything else for that matter), onions with cabbages, pole beans with corn.

A good space-saving idea is what I call multi-cropping. It works particularly well for

These young heads of lettuce were planted in a pattern to get the most production out of the space. They are a foot apart in each direction, but could be squeezed even a little closer.

a salad garden where, in one row the width of a garden rake (15 to 16 inches), I plant five crops together: radishes, onions, lettuce, carrots or beets, and spinach. Don't plant carrots

In wet areas or heavy clay soils where water stands after a rain, you can create raised beds like these. These work particularly well for getting spring crops in early. Even root crops will grow in wet areas on raised beds.

and beets together, because they both expand underground. You can plant carrots in half the row and beets in the other half. You can make these rows twice as wide if you want to. Add a splash of color by planting several different colored lettuce varieties. Sometimes I plant broccoli plants in the middle of these multi-plantings. As they grow, they provide shade for the greens, and the greens make a living mulch for the broccoli. Harvest whenever there is something ready to eat and you'll make room for the other crops to expand. You'll find more on multi-cropping in Chapter 6.

Plan for Success

Good garden planning pays off all season long. Once your garden is up and growing, it's too late to correct any major mistakes!

1. Know the dates of your last frost in the spring and first frost in the fall (see page 10). The number of days between these dates will tell you whether crops will mature in your area, and when to plant succession crops.

2. Think about which plants are short and which are tall, and plan your garden so that tall plants don't rob short ones of the sun . . . or so that they provide shade against the midsummer heat.

3. Use seed catalogs to gather information. Choose varieties that do well in your area.

GARDENING HAND TOOLS

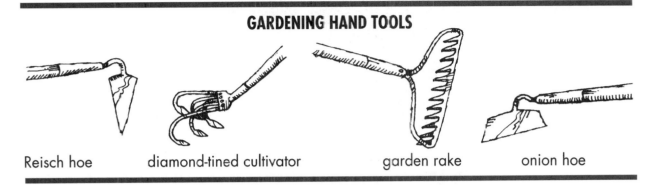

Reisch hoe   diamond-tined cultivator   garden rake   onion hoe

4. Buy seeds early for midsummer succession crops.

5. Plan your garden with wide rows and multi-plantings to make the most of the space you have.

6. Don't be afraid to mix flowers and vegetables, even in the front yard.

Many expert gardeners keep a ring binder or file near the garden tools. It contains the garden plan along with planting and harvest dates, notes on varieties planted, and reminders for next season. Some note rainfall and weather conditions. A record of your garden will help you to rotate crops each season, which is a good idea to help control insects. Some gardeners even cut up the seed catalogs and use the plant descriptions as part of their permanent gardening notes.

So plan in winter and enjoy the fruits of your planning in summer. That's really stretching the season!

Tooling Up

The vegetable gardener can get along with a very small investment in basic hand tools. If you are a homeowner you may have most of them already. It does pay to buy substantial tools once, not cheap tools over and over. For example, I have seen spades that fold in the middle when digging clay soils and anvil pruners with light blades that bend when faced with

a hardwood branch.

Here are some essentials:

An iron garden rake. This is one of the most important tools you'll use in your garden. A 15- or 16-inch-wide garden rake is a must for leveling seedbeds, making wide rows, building raised beds, thinning seedlings, spreading or removing mulches, and generally cleaning up.

Two hoes. A large hoe with a flat head 5 or 6 inches wide is good for tamping down seeds in raised beds, hilling, and chopping off weeds that have gotten out of control. A hoe with a small sharp head—sometimes called an "onion hoe"—is good for cultivating and weeding around plants as they grow and for making furrows for planting. For this I use either a Reisch hoe, which has a pointed, sharply triangular head, or a finger hoe, which has a head about the size of a man's index finger.

A spade. A solid, long-handled spade will turn your garden over in the spring and fall, turn in crops for succession planting, make a hole wherever you need it, and dig worms when it's time to go fishing.

A trowel or small digging tool. You'll use your trowel when you dig little holes to set out transplants.

A watering can. Especially useful in small gardens, you'll need a watering can to drench

This is my tool shed. You won't need nearly so many tools to garden successfully, but I also do a lot of testing and research.

Tool Trouble Spots

Most of the problems I've had with tools are the result of two shortcomings. One, the metal used in the tool is too light for the job. This is the spade that folds, the pruner blade that twists under stress, the trowel that bends where the metal enters the handle. The second problem is tool heads that come off because the head and the handle or shaft are not securely attached. Beware of tools that do not have a pin through the shaft that holds the head on. Some cheap tools simply have a piece of the metal head pounded into a hole in a wooden handle. Before you buy, twist the tool head at the handle to see if it is loose. If it is loose in the store, you can be sure it will be a disappointment. On the other hand, the heaviest tool isn't always the best one for you to own, either—especially if it is so heavy you avoid using it.

transplants, water seedbeds, and soak a plant that is suffering from summer's heat. You can buy inexpensive plastic ones, but a good galvanized metal watering can will pay off in the long run.

Odds and ends. Work gloves, a pocket-knife, a ball of garden twine, some wooden stakes for marking rows. A hose and sprinkler will also come in handy. You'll need a pail or two for handling lime, fertilizer, and so on. Recycled plastic buckets with lids are handy for storing things.

Tools to add. A spading fork will come in handy for digging potatoes and carrots at harvest time. A wheelbarrow or garden cart is a great labor-saving device for many tasks around the house in addition to gardening. A hand pruner is useful as the garden begins to grow, sprawl, and produce crops to harvest, as well as for general landscape maintenance.

Making Tools Last

Don't leave tools outside to rust and have the wood grain separate. Before putting tools away in the fall, rub the wooden handles with vegetable oil from the kitchen. Then clean the dirt off the metal parts and wipe them down with oil as well. (This is an excellent way to reuse motor oil that you've drained from your car or power equipment.) This will help to prevent rust. Sharpen your hand tools regularly and they will be much more efficient.

CHAPTER 2

SUCCESS
STARTS FROM THE GROUND UP

IN GARDENING, everything starts with the soil. Healthy soil produces plants that give you big yields and that resist damage from insects and disease.

It is through soil building that a gardener becomes a true steward of the earth, leaving it better than he or she found it. You can start building the soil with the very first garden you plant and make it better and more productive with each passing year.

The best thing a gardener can do to build soil is to add organic matter—things that are, or once were, plant material. People were amazed when I bet that I could grow a garden right in my gravel driveway. But I grew a very nice little garden in the driveway and all I did was add a lot of compost, which is decomposed organic matter. The point is: you can garden almost anywhere if you add plenty of organic matter.

Where do you find organic matter for your garden?

Here are some common kinds of organic matter:

🍎 *Manure* is plant material that has been run through a living compost machine like a horse, cow, sheep, rabbit, or chicken.

🍎 Homemade *compost* is one of the best

This very productive little garden was grown as a bet in my gravel driveway. It is just the size of my car. The secret ingredient in this garden is lots of compost dumped and mixed right on top of the gravel. The point is, you can garden almost anywhere—even in poor soil.

fertilizers you can make, and it is so important there is a whole chapter devoted to it beginning on page 23.

☙ *Peat moss* comes from thousands of years of plant buildup and decay that began when the glaciers retreated from the earth's northern latitudes.

☙ *Autumn leaves, grass clippings, vegetable wastes* from your kitchen, and nearly everything that has grown in your garden should be broken down and returned to the garden.

☙ *Crops* can actually be planted just to be turned into the soil to improve it. These crops are called "green manures." This is a good thing to know if you must skip one gardening season and don't want your garden to grow up into weeds. Plant a green manure to improve the soil and choke off weeds. For more in-depth information on green manures, see page 168 in the section called Scaling Up at the back of this book.

What Kind of Soil Do You Have?

Very few gardeners start out with the rich, sandy loam that is considered ideal for gardening. In most parts of the country you can find extremely different kinds of soil within a few miles of each other. You might have heavy clay soil, while a few miles away the gardeners are dealing with thin, sandy soil. If you have clay it will stay as a thick clump with clearly defined edges when you turn it over with a spade. Water will stand on it instead of soaking in. It will warm up very slowly in the spring. Sandy soil has just the opposite characteristics. It crumbles easily, it will look dry a few hours after a rain, and it warms up quickly.

The one thing clay and sand have in common is that they both improve with the addition of organic matter. Clay is made up of tiny flat particles, so small you may not be able to see them without a magnifying glass. They are like a deck of cards sliding around on each other. Sand, on the other hand, is composed of large, rough particles you can see very clearly. In the middle range is silt. What we all would like to have is soil made up of a mixture of particle sizes. That would give us sandy loam.

Organic matter begins to improve the soil immediately. In sandy soils it is like a binder that holds it together and absorbs water. In clay, organic matter becomes tiny wedges that separate the discs and allow the soil to breathe.

Work with Nature to Build Soil

Dirt is what you find in the corners of your house or under the bed when you don't clean very often. Soil is different. Soil is alive! Each cubic inch of good garden soil contains millions of microorganisms too small to see. It also can contain a variety of larger living things, including one of the gardener's best pals, the earthworm. The earthworm feeds on raw, undigested vegetable matter and turns it into rich worm manure called "castings."

In the gradual process of consuming and decomposing the dead plant and animal remains, the soil organisms cause the release of valuable minerals and trace elements in a form that plant roots can absorb.

Organic matter is the food supply for healthy soil life activity. Organic matter may actually vanish into the soil faster after the first year of soil building because a growing army of soil life is breaking it down.

Gardeners love humus, and can never get enough of it. Humus is organic matter in its final stage of decomposition. It gives soil a good, spongy texture and allows the necessary circulation of air to plant roots. It helps the plant retain and absorb the right amount of moisture. And it helps break up heavy clay soils and hold together light sandy soils.

Soil that is not regularly refueled with organic matter can become lifeless and unable to support plants, like a desert. Earthworms leave to search for food somewhere else. Minerals and nutrients stay locked up in soil particles, unavailable for plant growth. Decomposing organic matter, you see, produces weak carbonic acids which help dissolve soil nutrients.

Chemical fertilizers can be poured on in huge quantities, but they won't do a thing for the soil texture or for the soil-life population in the long run. In fact, they can actually destroy soil life. Commercial growers are often locked into the use of chemical fertilizers because of the demand to maximize production, like a factory. Home gardeners, though, can work with the processes of nature to build soil.

Your Soil's Strong and Weak Points

Once you understand the importance of organic matter, the second thing to understand is your soil's strengths and weaknesses for gardening purposes. Plants need a certain level of acidity for optimum growth, as well as a balance of basic fertilizers like nitrogen, phosphates, and potash. As you begin to understand your soil, you'll understand how important it is to achieve and maintain this proper balance.

How to Add Organic Matter

Here are some of the most common ways to add organic matter to your soil:

1. You can buy it in packaged form.

No matter what kind of soil you have, it can be improved with the addition of organic matter like compost. The vegetable material in the lower hand has not decomposed quite as much as that above. Microorganisms in the soil feed on organic matter and break it down into a form your plants can use. Organic matter helps them multiply.

Turning plant material back into the soil after its growing season both builds soil and prevents insects and diseases from setting up housekeeping.

Peat moss and dehydrated manures can be worked into your garden. Peat moss absorbs up to 20 times its weight in water, so it is good to work into the soil if you are concerned about it drying out. It breaks down very slowly, which is good, but contains almost no nutrients. A 50–50 mixture of peat moss and compost gives you the best of both worlds—moisture retention and nutrients.

2. You can chop and till all garden residues and weeds back into your soil.

3. You can buy bales of marsh hay or straw, use it for mulch, then turn it into your garden at the end of the season. Look carefully at bales of hay or straw before buying them. You want to avoid bringing seeds into your garden. Straw

An inexpensive exercise machine like a spade may be all you need to turn over your garden, especially if it is small.

should be clean, since it is the stalks of grain after the head has been harvested. But some kinds of straw are better than others. Inspect it. Straw breaks down slowly and uses up nitrogen in the process.

4. You can get wastes from canneries, cider mills, or other processors, usually free for the taking. Sawdust is not great for garden use. Like straw, it breaks down slowly and uses up nitrogen in the process. If you're in doubt about what to bring in, you can use my rule of thumb: If an earthworm wouldn't eat this, I won't put it in the garden.

5. You can work in all kinds of animal manures, household vegetable garbage, leaves, and grass clippings. Fresh manures can be worked into the garden a few weeks ahead of planting time, but should not be used directly on plants, since they contain acids that can harm your plants. Garbage can be buried in the garden, and earthworms will dispose of it. (Be sure to include coffee grounds.) Leaves, if turned in, will break down over the winter. Grass clippings should be allowed to dry or they turn into a heavy, smelly, moldy mass. If you are using herbicides on your lawn on a regular basis, avoid using fresh grass clippings. Broadleaf weed killer can't tell the difference between a dandelion and a vegetable plant. Let clippings dry out for two weeks to allow the herbicides to break down. Then ask yourself, do you really need those herbicides on your lawn?

6. Compost. Everything in number 5

above will be in better shape to be worked into the garden if it is composted first. The next chapter is devoted to composting.

7. Grow various crops as "green manures" strictly for their soil-improving benefits, then chop and till them into the soil. This is an excellent long-term soil building practice, and is covered in a separate section beginning on page 168.

Starting a New Garden

Most people begin their new gardens in the spring when gardening fever is in the air. But the best time to start a new garden is in the fall. You do just about the same things, but if you begin in the fall nature has a little more time to work with you. Here are some of the things you'll want to do after you've done the planning and site selection we talked about earlier.

Turn the soil over to create a clear space for planting. Chances are, a new garden site will be created out of a patch of lawn or will have to be cleared of weeds or other wild growth. In a small plot, just use a spade to dig in and turn the clumps upside down so the grass or weeds point down and their roots point up. Or you can skin the sod off with a flat garden spade. If you have a tiller, run it over and over the spot until it is well turned in. You might try checking with a garden center or tiller dealer to see if you can hire someone to come over and till it for you. A rental center might

If you know ahead of time that you're going to start a new garden next year, you can use a shortcut to prepare the area. All summer long, pile yard wastes, including branches of trees you've trimmed, on the area that will be your garden. The shade will kill off anything currently growing and earthworms will be at work under the pile turning the material into rich earth. Remove the material to your compost pile when you're ready to turn the garden over. The soil should be rich and easy to work.

In gardening, everything springs from the health of your soil. A soil test involves taking samples from several locations, mixing them together, and either analyzing them yourself with a simple kit or sending them away for professional analysis. Inexpensive soil test kits are available at garden centers.

have a tiller you can rent. This makes sense for a larger garden. For a small garden, just think of your spade as a Nautilus machine and be happy you don't have to pay membership fees to a gym to get such good exercise. Anything you remove from the garden—weeds, clumps, sod—should go straight into your compost pile. After a few days, the earthworms will be busy turning the grass and weeds—now underground—into soil. The advantage of starting in the fall is that there will be much more time for the grass to break down into soil. By turning it over a second time in the spring before you plant you reduce the chances of any remaining weeds or growth making an unwanted comeback.

Preparing the Soil for Planting

In the spring, begin preparing your soil as early as possible. But don't start work if the soil is still soggy from melting snow and ice or spring rains. When the ground is dry enough to work, you can pick up a clod and easily break it apart with your thumbs. Soil that is too wet won't break apart so easily. If the soil is already turned over from the fall, step into the garden. If you leave a shiny, wet footprint it is still too early.

Be sure to take a soil test. The best time for this is in the fall, but a spring test is better than no test at all. This is the sure-fire way to get to know your soil's strengths and weaknesses. Check with your garden center to find out what your choices are for testing the soil. These will range from a simple do-it-yourself kit to test acidity, all the way to a mail-back kit that can be sent to the Extension Service at your state university for a detailed soil analysis. There are also soil-testing labs that charge a little more. They will report back on the soil's acidity or alkalinity (pH), nitrogen,

In most of the eastern United States and parts of the Far West, gardeners add lime to the soil to achieve a balance between acidity and alkalinity that encourages plant growth. It can be broadcast onto the garden by hand and raked in.

phosphorus, potassium, and soil texture. They will also make recommendations on how to improve the soil. If you want recommendations on organic improvements, ask for them, or you will most likely get chemical fertilizer suggestions. Some tests go into greater detail and get into nutrients like magnesium and calcium. Again, fall is a good time to plan ahead and have the soil tested. Labs aren't as busy, and if you do have to add things like lime to improve pH, you can add it in the fall, since lime breaks down slowly. Soil tests are a lot like physicals. People can think of a lot of reasons not to take the time, but often they turn up simple problems that can be easily corrected to prevent bigger problems later on.

Control pH with Lime or Sulphur

Think of pH as a kind of thermometer that goes from 1 to 14 in measuring soils' acidity or alkalinity. Just as people are most comfortable with temperatures in the mid-60s to mid-70s, most of your garden vegetables will do best with a soil acidity in the range of 6.3 to 7. The lower the number, the more acid the soil. The higher the number, the more alkaline it is.

In the eastern United States gardeners often add lime to their soil to raise the pH. In the West, they often add sulphur to the soil to lower the pH.

Without a balanced soil pH, somewhere near neutral, fertilizers will not work. A test of 6.3 is slightly acid, and you will not need to add lime. A test of 7 is neutral. Simple do-it-yourself test kits for pH are available at many garden centers.

If you use my old standby formula, I think you eastern gardeners can avoid trouble with soil pH. Spread one 10-quart bucket of lime on every 1,000 square feet of garden space. If

Be sure to turn your garden over one more time the day you plant it. This will expose weed seeds to the air and knock down those that are just germinating. It really helps to control weeds.

OPTIMUM PH RANGE FOR VEGETABLE CROPS

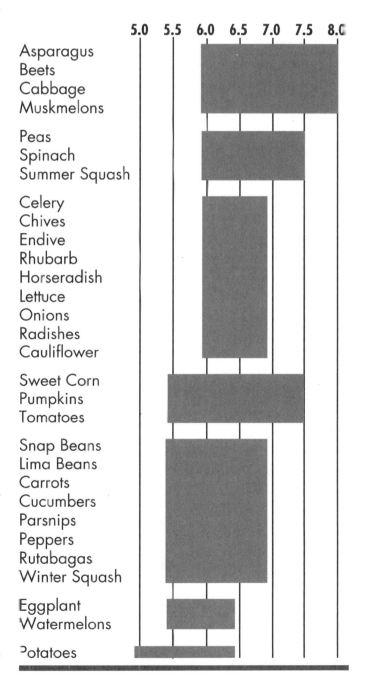

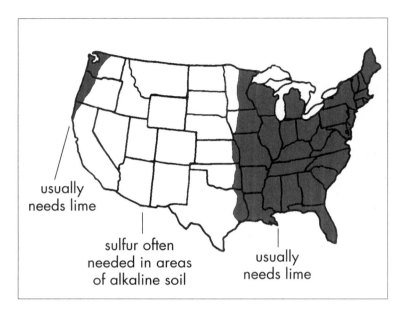

usually
needs lime

sulfur often
needed in areas
of alkaline soil

usually
needs lime

pers and blueberries are examples. And don't put too much lime on your potato patch. Potatoes do better in a slightly acid soil.

Wood Ashes

If you have a fireplace or have access to wood ashes, you can use them as a substitute for lime, but they should be used sparingly. Spread at about the same rate you would for lime, or one 10-quart bucket per 1,000 square feet of garden. They are also useful around plants bothered by slugs. Wood ashes dissolve faster than lime and raise the soil pH faster. If you spread ashes each spring, use about two pounds per 100 square feet of garden. Hardwood ashes have more nutrients than softwood ashes.

you do this once every three or four years, your soil should stay pretty much within the 6.3 to 7 range. Do a pH test every once in a while just to be sure.

Some plants actually like acid soil. Pep-

CHAPTER 3

COMPOST:
THE DO-IT-YOURSELF FERTILIZER

GARDEN COMPOST is a mixture of various kinds of decomposed organic matter. In a way, it is a "synthetic manure," every bit as rich and fertile as the real thing, and in some ways better.

There are probably as many ways to make compost as there are recipes for salad. Everyone does it a little differently. I won't try to tell you exactly how to do it; you should develop some of your own techniques. I will just make a few general suggestions and describe a composting method that I have helped to develop. My method is for people who don't generate a huge amount of garbage, who don't have enough land to have a lot of excess organic matter, and who like to keep their places looking neat and attractive.

You can make compost in an open pile, but some kind of container keeps things better organized. The simplest compost containers are round, wire cages or boxes made out of slats of wood. The main purpose of a compost pile—in or out of a container—is to mix moisture, air, and organic matter in equal amounts so

that the organic matter will become humus as quickly as possible. In other words, you are trying to get a mixture that is one-third air, one-third water, and one-third organic matter. No one expects these proportions to be perfect, naturally. This is just a rough formula.

Any compost system needs to be *activated*. In other words, you need to get the helpful bacteria and fungi working for you within the pile. My tests here in Vermont have proven to me that this should be done by adding some sort of protein-nitrogen substance. *Commercial fertilizer does not work as an activator.* The microorganisms you are trying to encourage do not seem to be interested in man-made nitrogen. It does not help the pile to decompose, and it does not help it to generate heat—an essential factor in successful composting.

Manure, rich soil, alfalfa meal, soybean meal, blood meal, bonemeal, cottonseed meal, and dry dog food are all sources of protein and nitrogen. Animals, of course, take in protein in many different forms and excrete a good deal of it in their manure. Blood meal, bonemeal,

Two or three wire compost bins allow you to turn and move material from one to the other as it decomposes. Air, moisture, and an activator are needed to break down organic matter into compost. Activators feed the microorganisms and speed up decomposition.

and hoof and horn meal are types of animal matter that always contain protein. Alfalfa meal and soybean meal come from legumes, so both contain much protein and a lot of nitrogen. Good soil is rich in protein and nitrogen, as is cottonseed meal. The higher the protein content in the activator, the more efficiently the pile will work and the richer your compost will be.

Begin by collecting whatever organic material you have. Next, build yourself a wire cage or box large enough to hold all of this material and more. Put a few leaves in the container, throw on some garbage, and sprinkle in a handful of activator. Then add a little of some different kind of material, such as grass clippings, and add water—just enough so that the leaves and grass feel like a damp sponge. Don't soak it. Then add another two or three handfuls of activator, and sprinkle on more water. Keep building up layers of materials in

this way until the container is full. If you can't fill the whole thing up right away, add more organic matter to the pile as you get it.

If you have so much organic matter that you don't know what to do with it all, and have access to a supply of manure, you can go into composting on a larger scale. You could build a 5-foot pile in a container that is as large as 4 or 5 feet square. Begin layering your pile just as before. Throw in some old hay, leaves, or weeds. Then put in a thinner layer of manure and maybe a little soil, and add water. Keep building the pile until you run out of materials or until the container is filled.

Turning and mixing the materials every once in a while is a very important step. Don't forget that the pile needs oxygen. Microbes at work in the material need to breathe if they are to function properly. Turning and mixing the materials with a pitchfork lets more air into

COMPOST ORGANIZERS CAN BE MADE OF DIFFERENT MATERIALS AND IN VARIOUS SHAPES

Concrete-block bin

Wire-mesh bin

Whichever method you choose to contain your compost, remember to allow for air circulation within the pile. In the concrete-block bin above, perforated plastic piping inserted between blocks near the bottom of the pile allows air circulation. If you build a simple wooden composting system like the one at the right, be sure to leave some space between the horizontal slats.

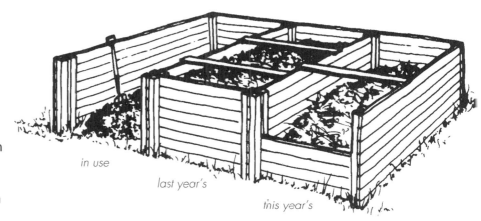

in use

last year's

this year's

the pile. If the pile suddenly starts to smell bad, the wrong type of bacteria and fungi have taken over inside. This is a sure sign that the pile needs to be turned. You shouldn't have to do this more often than once every several weeks.

Don't expect your compost pile to produce rich, black humus which is perfectly decomposed—unless, of course, you plan to let it sit for years. It takes a long time for things like leaves and cornstalks to break down completely. Don't worry if some of the ingredients are not completely rotted. The compost you have made is still good stuff to use in your garden, especially under transplants. The final

decomposition will take place in the soil itself. In the meantime, your plants will be getting lots of nourishment. Partly decayed compost is good fertilizer, because it releases its nutrients to the plants gradually, not all in one shot.

How to Make a Simple Wire-Mesh Compost Bin

1. Take a strip of wire mesh 2 or 3 feet wide by 9 feet long. Fasten the ends together to form a circular compost cage.
2. Place a 2- to 6-inch-thick layer of coarse material, such as leaves, hay, or weeds, in the bottom.

The well-made compost pile.

3. Sprinkle on a large handful of an activator, rich in nitrogen and protein, thoroughly covering the coarse material. You can use alfalfa meal, soybean meal, cottonseed meal, bonemeal, or other high-protein meal. *Commercial fertilizers will not work.*

4. Continue building the compost pile by alternating layers of coarse material and meal.

5. Moisten the pile thoroughly. Don't oversoak. Most failures are due to the pile's being too dry or too wet.

6. Compact the outer edges of the pile. **Important:** The center must remain loose to allow air to penetrate the pile. The composting process depends upon the meal, coarse material, moisture, and air all coming in contact with each other.

If the pile is made correctly, the temperature will reach 140° to 150°F. (60°

to 65°C.) in several days.

In about one or two weeks, turn the pile, mixing the materials together. Fork outside dry material into the center of the pile. Moisten the pile again if it's too dry. The heating process will start up again. Compost is ready to use when the pile stops heating in four to five weeks.

7. To turn the pile, remove the wire cage by placing your foot on the pile and lifting off the wire. Fork the material back into the empty cage.

Lots of people like to add lime to their compost piles. I have always believed that lime slows down the bacterial action in the pile, but I have never seen this proven anywhere. I usually add lime after the compost is removed from the pile and before I use it in the garden. If you have used many different types of material, you don't have to worry about adding lime. Your compost should naturally develop a fairly neutral pH.

Many people believe that compost made out of oak leaves or pine needles will be acidic, and this is true. But experiments in Connecticut and Missouri have proven that tilling oak leaves and pine residues directly into the garden will not lower the soil's pH. It may be wise to have a sample of your compost analyzed. If it really is acidic, treat it with lime.

It is a good idea to grind extremely coarse material before you put it in the compost pile. This exposes more surface area to bacterial action and helps speed up the decomposition. But grinding things so fine that they tend to pack down may hinder air circulation within the pile. If everything is going to be chopped up, you'd better insert some sort of ventilation pipes to get air into the inner parts of the pile.

Are there any materials that you should not put in a compost pile? I am sure you know enough not to put in anything that will never decompose—nonbiodegradable things like plastic, glass, aluminum, and charcoal. Some people use meat scraps; these are fine if you have a very active pile that heats up to temperatures between 100° and 160°F. (38° to 71°C.). On the other hand, meat scraps can attract dogs and other carnivorous animals, like raccoons. These creatures will tear up your pile and make a mess. Protect it from them by putting a strong wire screen over the top. Or leave out the meat scraps.

Everyone can compost garbage, even if they have no additional organic matter to add to it. You can do this in a small container that is only 2 or 3 feet in diameter. I have made

Compost fertilizes plants and improves soil. It can be turned into the soil before it is completely broken down. Earthworms and soil life will finish the job. Put compost in the rows, hills, and seedbeds with the plants where it will do the most good.

garbage compost by adding peat moss, alfalfa meal, and water to ordinary garbage. I could have used soybean meal, blood meal, or bonemeal just as well, I'm sure. The final product of this mixture was a wonderfully rich compost which I added to my potting soil. The seedlings that grew in it turned out to be some of the best I have ever had.

Good Things to Put into Your Compost Pile

As more and more landfills refuse to accept yard wastes, a compost pile suddenly makes sense even to people who are not devoted gardeners. Grass clippings, leaves, and vegetable wastes from the kitchen are not the only things for the compost pile, however. If you think of your compost pile as your own private fertilizer factory, you'll soon be searching for more materials to add.

A covered plastic pail under the kitchen sink is a good way to collect all the things you trim and cut from your vegetables, as well as coffee grounds and even the filters. Avoid meat or bones, since they can smell and attract pests, and since grease doesn't compost well. Don't buy a bucket; ask for one at a donut shop, because fillings are shipped in plastic buckets that can't be used again. Supermarkets may have buckets or fish boxes, which are excellent for storing gardening materials. Or, look for a building site where they are putting up wallboard. The joint compound comes in very heavy-duty plastic buckets with tight lids.

RE-HARVEST YOUR FERTILIZERS

All the vegetable wastes you are sending down the garbage disposal to tax our sewage treatment plants should be turned into fertilizer in the compost pile. After you harvest your vegetables from the garden, why send nutrients to the landfill or down the drain to cause problems? Recycle them in compost. You'll also be recycling the soil you used to grow them in the first place.

Things to Add to Your Compost Pile Include:

Alfalfa meal and hay (the meal will activate the pile)
Algae (pond weeds)
Apple pomace (cider press waste)
Ashes (wood, not coal. Sprinkle lightly between layers, don't add ashes in big clumps)
Banana skins (as well as all fruit and vegetable peels, stalks, and foliage)
Bean shells and stalks
Bird cage cleanings
Broccoli stalks (shred, cut, or pound soft with a mallet)
Buckwheat hulls or straw
Cabbage stalks and leaves
Cocoa hulls
Cat litter (prophyllite, alfalfa pellets, or vermiculite before the cat has used it. Alfalfa pellets will help activate the pile)
Citrus wastes and rinds
Clover
Coffee wastes and grounds
Corn cobs (shred or chop)
Corn stalks (shred or chop)
Cottonseed hulls
Cotton waste ("gin trash")
Cowpeas

Cucumber vines (unless they are diseased or insect-infected)
Dog food (dry dog food is a nitrogen/protein activator)
Dolomite
Earthworms
Eelgrass
Eggshells (grind or crush)
Fish scraps (bury in the center of the pile)
Flowers
Grape pomace (winery waste)
Granite dust
Grass clippings (let dry first and use in thin layers between other materials; a thick mass will be a mess)
Greensand
Hay (mixed grasses or salt marsh hay)
Hedge clippings
Hops (brewery waste)
Kelp (seaweed)
Leaf mold
Leaves
Lettuce
Lime (agricultural)
Limestone (ground)
Milk (sour)

Muck

Melon wastes (vines, leaves, and rinds, unless diseased or infested)

Oat straw

Olive residues

Pea pods and vines

Peanut hulls

Peat moss

Phosphate rock

Pine needles (use sparingly; they are acidic and break down slowly)

Potash rock

Potato wastes (skins, etc.; watch out for insect-infested vines)

Rhubarb leaves

Rice hulls

Shells (ground clam, crab, lobster, mussel, and oyster)

Sod and soil removed from other areas

Soybean straw

Sphagnum moss

Sugar cane residue (bagasse)

Tea leaves

Vetch

Weeds (even with seeds, which will be killed as the pile heats up)

Wheat straw

Natural Activators

Making compost is a little like making yogurt. You need to get some good bacteria working for you to make it happen. Soil and existing compost are good activators. Here are some others:

Alfalfa meal
(The best activator. Sold as "Litter Green" kitty litter or pelletized as rabbit food. Sometimes sold in 50-pound bags at feed stores. Try a place that sells feed for horses.)

Blood meal

Bonemeal

Cottonseed meal

Dry dog food

Fish meal

Hoof meal

Horn meal

Manure

Questionable Materials for the Compost Pile

Newspapers. Black-and-white sections could be all right if shredded, but they break down slowly. A better use might be to mulch garden walkways with thick sections and cover it with marsh hay or straw for appearance's sake and to prevent the papers from blowing around.

Sludge. In some parts of the world human waste has been used for years as compost. Activated sludge is different from digested sludge. I avoid it in vegetable gardens simply because the potential risk exceeds the reward when there are so many other materials around to compost. However, sludge can be used on lawns and flower beds and returned to the vegetable garden after clippings and flowers are composted.

Weeds. Green weeds are fine to compost before seeds ripen. Weeds with seeds are fine if you do your compost correctly and it heats up enough to kill the weed seeds.

Corncobs, broccoli stalks, leaves. These will break down gradually in a compost pile, but they're best if chopped or shredded. Another answer is to turn them into the soil or bury them in a trench where they are in contact with a super activator—the soil.

Alfalfa Meal: The Organic Gardener's Secret Weapon

Although alfalfa is one of the most common of the field crops, it is just beginning to be discovered by organic gardeners and the people who make organic fertilizers.

Alfalfa is usually grown to be baled as hay, but it is also ground up and sold as meal or pressed into pellets for a variety of uses, including rabbit food and kitty litter.

I discovered its benefits as a fertilizer by accident. One autumn I spread alfalfa hay as mulch on one half of a berry patch and straw on the other half. When I uncovered the patch the following spring, the berry plants seemed bigger, greener, and healthier where I had used the alfalfa hay. During the next year, I used alfalfa meal directly as a fertilizer and spread a swath across the garden and mixed it into the soil. As the plants grew, I could actually see the difference where I had applied the alfalfa meal.

Why does alfalfa meal work as a fertilizer?

First of all, it is a legume—one of the plants that can take nitrogen from the air (after all, nitrogen is a gas) and fix it onto its roots, thereby turning it into a form that plants can use in the soil.

Second, alfalfa roots travel deep into the soil—up to 40 feet deep—to pick up trace minerals far below the surface.

Third, in the 1970s researchers found that alfalfa contains *triacontanol*, a primary growth stimulant that can give as much as a 10 to 15 percent greater harvest.

There is an additional benefit to using alfalfa meal in the garden: it is a relatively inexpensive source of nitrogen. Man-made nitrogen requires a lot of energy to produce and drains our natural resources. And the plants are able to use only a small percentage of the chemical fertilizers that are applied to them.

Sources

Farm supply stores are a good place to start looking for alfalfa meal. It is sold in 50-pound bags that typically cost less than $10. It may also be found in stores catering to horse owners. Check out pelletized rabbit food . . . it may be all alfalfa.

Another source is the supermarket. Litter Green kitty litter is alfalfa pellets. Other brands may be clay compounds. Check the bag for contents. Pelletized alfalfa is fine to use on your garden; just use smaller amounts than you would of alfalfa meal.

Finally, some commercially available organic garden fertilizers may contain alfalfa meal. Again, check the bags of these fertilizers for contents.

Application

Alfalfa meal is useful as both a fertilizer and an activator for your compost pile. (Kitty litter **should not** be used in the cat box first).

In the spring, sprinkle alfalfa meal or pellets over the garden soil before planting, and then mix it into the top 3 or 4 inches of soil.

As crops begin to blossom, side-dress each plant with a couple of tablespoons of alfalfa meal. Mix the meal with the soil so it doesn't blow away and water the plant to activate the side dressing.

On your compost pile, sprinkle a thin layer of alfalfa meal on each new layer of organic material you add. It will help the pile decompose faster and will fortify it with the trace minerals necessary for good plant growth.

THE CHEMICAL MERRY-GO-ROUND

A discovery by the German chemist Justus von Liebig in the 19th century put agriculture on a merry-go-round that we are still riding today.

Von Liebig demonstrated that nitrogen, phosphorus, and potassium are the three basic elements necessary for plant growth. At the time, horse manure was widely available, and the impact of his discovery was not immediately felt. But as the motor vehicle replaced the horse, agriculture turned to chemical fertilizers.

Von Liebig didn't know about soil bacteria and soil life or about trace minerals, but the merry-go-round was up and running. It started out well enough. Chemically fertilized crops *do* grow lush . . . at first. But over the years they began to lack resistance to pests and diseases. So pesticides and fungicides were developed to combat the insects and diseases. These pests, in time, developed resistance to the chemicals, and new chemicals had to be invented to control them.

Round and round it goes, and now we are seeing evidence that some pesticides are harmful to people as well as pests. They even appear to harm the soil life itself, making soil less productive and causing it to require a steady diet of chemical fertilizers. Maybe we have outsmarted ourselves.

Using organic methods, the home gardener can avoid the merry-go-round of chemical usage, build healthier and more fertile soil, and exercise control over what he or she puts on the table for the family.

CHAPTER 4
PICKING
THE RIGHT VARIETIES

Your planning with the seed catalog can pay off when you go to the garden center in the spring. With a little luck you can save money by buying the varieties you've selected in bulk.

BUY YOUR SEED from reputable seed companies. Most of us get only one whack at the gardening season, so good seeds are a must. Plant seed from packets that have this year's date printed on them, and, if you can, from packs that have a guaranteed germination percentage. There is nothing more discouraging than planting old seeds and having them not come up. You can lose as much as two weeks of the gardening year this way.

Because there is so much emphasis on organic gardening these days, most seeds are no longer treated with fungicides. In the past, these chemicals prevented the fungus that causes damping-off from destroying your seedlings. In years when spring is particularly wet, you may have a problem with damping-off, which appears as wilting or rotting in young seedlings. If you plant in wide rows you will have enough seeds in the ground to make sure you have a harvest even with some problems.

Mail-Order Seed Companies

Seed catalogs are great shopping fun, but they make comparison buying impossible. Each company likes to give newly developed varieties its own unique brand names. Another company may have a very similar variety— or even the same variety—but call it by a different name. Some nationally known varieties, which are usually available at local seed stores, are sold under different names by mail-order companies.

But seed shopping by mail does have a lot of advantages. The catalogs almost always offer a better, larger selection than local stores. And they give a description of the advantages— though seldom any disadvantages—of each variety. Plus it's so exciting to get a boxful of seeds in the mail when the last snow is still on the ground.

Following is a short list of suggested mail-order seed companies from which to make your selections. All are reputable, and you'll get good service.

Abundant Life Seed
   Foundation
P.O. Box 772
Port Townsend, WA 98368

Burgess Seed & Plant Co.
905 Four Seasons Road
Bloomington, IL 61701

W. Atlee Burpee Co.
300 Park Avenue
Warminster, PA 18991

Comstock, Ferre & Co.
263 Main Street
Wethersfield, CT 06109

The Cook's Garden
P.O. Box 65
Londonderry, VT 05148

William Dam Seeds, Ltd.
Box 8400
Dundas, Ontario
L9H 6M1, Canada

Farmer Seed & Nursery
1706 Morrissey Drive
Bloomington, IL 61704

Garden City Seeds
P.O. Box 297
Victor, MT 59875

Gurney Seed & Nursery Co.
110 Capitol Street
Yankton, SD 57078

Harris Seeds
60 Saginaw Drive
Rochester, NY 14623

Le Jardin Du Gourmet
West Danville, VT 05873

Johnny's Selected Seeds
305 Foss Hill Road
Albion, ME 04910

J.W. Jung Seed Co.
335 South High Street
Randolph, WI 53957

Earl May Seed & Nursery
208 North Elm
Shenandoah, IA 51603

J.E. Miller Nurseries, Inc.
5060 West Lake Road
Canandaigua, NY 14424

(*Strawberries, horseradish, asparagus, rhubarb*)

George W. Park Seed Co.
P.O. Box 31
Greenwood, SC 29648-0031

Rayner Brothers, Inc.
P.O. Box 1617
Salisbury, MD 21801

(*Strawberries, asparagus, rhubarb*)

Richters Herb Catalogue
Box 26
Goodwood, Ontario
L0C 1A0, Canada

Seeds Blüm
Idaho City Stage
Boise, ID 83706

Shepherd's Garden Seeds
7389 West Zayante Road
Felton, CA 95018

Southern Exposure Seed
    Exchange
P.O. Box 158
North Garden, VA 22959

Stark Brothers Nurseries
Highway 54
Louisiana, MO 63353

(Rhubarb, strawberries, asparagus)

Stokes Seeds, Inc.
P.O. Box 548
Buffalo, NY 14240

Thompson & Morgan
P.O. Box 1308
Jackson, NJ 08527

Tomato Growers Supply Co.
P.O. Box 2237
Fort Myers, FL 33902

Vesey's Seeds Ltd.
P.O. Box 9000
Houlton, ME 04730

Which Varieties Are Right for You?

We wanted to find out which vegetable varieties were most successful in various parts of the country, so we sent letters to a sampling of state extension services and seed companies. In each letter, we included a list of eight vegetables—tomatoes, snap beans, corn, lima beans, cucumbers, peas, cantaloupes, and squash. We asked the recipients to name the three best varieties of each of these vegetables for their area and to list any miscellaneous local favorites.

Because our sample was small, our results were not conclusive. But they were interesting. To give you an example of the complexity of our results, see the map on page 36. We listed tomato-variety recommendations for many areas of the country. The varieties with the most "votes" were Betty Boy, Supersonic, Jet Star, Heinz 1350, New Yorker, Spring Giant, Moreton Hybrid, and Floradel. But, as you can see, many other varieties were also cited—so many that choosing among them is difficult and confusing. Some of the regional selections may be, at least partially, a reflection of the buying habits of the population or of the availability of certain varieties. The situation is made even more complex by the fact that the same variety is sometimes offered by two different companies under two different names. If your own favorite tomato variety is not recommended for your area, don't abandon it if it has done well for you. You might, however, like to experiment with some of the recommended varieties, too. Maybe you'll find a new favorite.

Below are the varieties most frequently cited in the seven other categories that we listed in the survey. Asterisked varieties are

If you leave the stalks on at harvest time you can store your onions in hanging bunches by braiding the stalks together like pigtails.

Not all carrots are the same. Here are mature Early French, Danvers, and Imperator varieties. Early French have a short growing season, the thick Danvers do well in clay soils, and the long, thin Imperator is good for thin and sandy soils.

Tiny Sweet 100's are among the best-tasting cherry tomatoes. They are good to use with dips and fresh in salads. They grow almost like bunches of grapes in a cluster. The plants grow throughout the season and can become very tall.

Different cukes for different purposes. On the right are slicers for use in salads and fresh eating. The smaller cukes on the left are for pickling, but they can also be eaten fresh.

At the other extreme, just one Beefsteak tomato weighs in at 3 pounds. (This one is cut in half.) These are excellent for slicing fresh. For sauces, a plum tomato like Roma is a good choice because it has more pulp and less water content.

outstanding favorites.

Snap Beans: Tendercrop*, Contender, Provider, Bush Blue Lake, Harvester.

Cucumbers: Marketmore 76, Pioneer, Poinsett*, Victory Hybrid, SMR Picklers.

Peas: Little Marvel*, Freezonian, Wando, Frosty, Progress No. 9, Patriot, Green Arrow.

Corn: Silver Queen*, Gold Cup, Spring Gold.

Lima Beans: Fordhook 242*, Henderson, Thaxter.

Cantaloupes: Burpee Hybrid*, Gold Star, Harper Hybrid.

Squash: Elite Zucchini, Summer Straightneck, Butternut, Buttercup, Early Prolific, Delicata.

POPULAR TOMATO VARIETIES

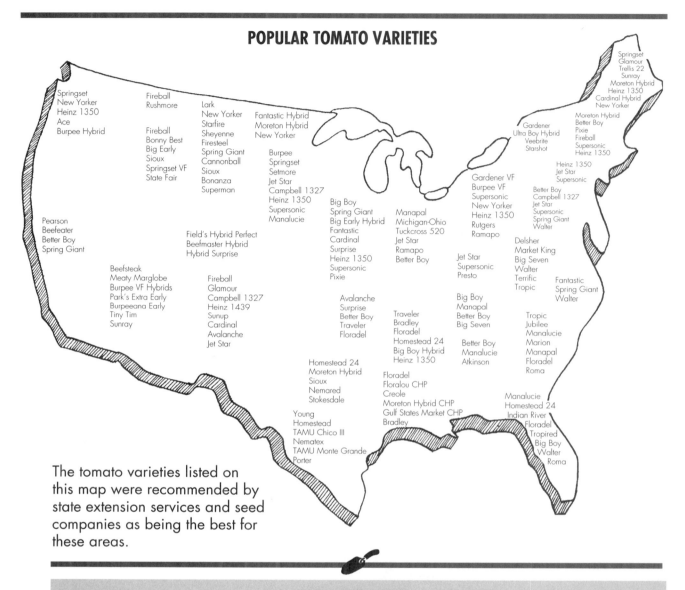

Springset
Glamour
Trellis 22
Sunray
Moreton Hybrid
Heinz 1350
Cardinal Hybrid
New Yorker

Springset
New Yorker
Heinz 1350
Ace
Burpee Hybrid

Fireball
Rushmore

Lark
New Yorker
Starfire
Sheyenne
Firesteel
Spring Giant
Cannonball
Sioux
Bonanza
Superman

Fantastic Hybrid
Moreton Hybrid
New Yorker

Fireball
Bonny Best
Big Early
Sioux
Springset VF
State Fair

Moreton Hybrid
Better Boy
Pixie
Fireball
Supersonic
Heinz 1350

Gardener
Ultra Boy Hybrid
Veebrite
Starshot

Burpee
Springset
Setmore
Jet Star
Campbell 1327
Heinz 1350
Supersonic
Manalucie

Heinz 1350
Jet Star
Supersonic

Gardener VF
Burpee VF
Supersonic
New Yorker
Heinz 1350
Rutgers
Ramapo

Better Boy
Campbell 1327
Jet Star
Supersonic
Spring Giant
Walter

Pearson
Beefeater
Better Boy
Spring Giant

Big Boy
Spring Giant
Big Early Hybrid
Fantastic
Cardinal
Surprise
Heinz 1350
Supersonic
Pixie

Manapal
Michigan-Ohio
Tuckcross 520
Jet Star
Ramapo
Better Boy

Delsher
Market King
Big Seven
Walter
Terrific
Tropic

Field's Hybrid Perfect
Beefmaster Hybrid
Hybrid Surprise

Jet Star
Supersonic
Presto

Fantastic
Spring Giant
Walter

Beefsteak
Meaty Marglobe
Burpee VF Hybrids
Park's Extra Early
Burpeeana Early
Tiny Tim
Sunray

Fireball
Glamour
Campbell 1327
Heinz 1439
Sunup
Cardinal
Avalanche
Jet Star

Avalanche
Surprise
Better Boy
Traveler
Floradel

Big Boy
Manapal
Better Boy
Big Seven

Tropic
Jubilee
Manalucie
Marion
Manapal
Floradel
Roma

Traveler
Bradley
Floradel
Homestead 24
Big Boy Hybrid
Heinz 1350

Better Boy
Manalucie
Atkinson

Homestead 24
Moreton Hybrid
Sioux
Nemared
Stokesdale

Floradel
Floralou CHP
Creole
Moreton Hybrid CHP
Gulf States Market CHP
Bradley

Manalucie
Homestead 24
Indian River
Floradel
Tropired
Big Boy
Walter
Roma

Young
Homestead
TAMU Chico III
Nematex
TAMU Monte Grande
Porter

The tomato varieties listed on this map were recommended by state extension services and seed companies as being the best for these areas.

STORING SEEDS

If you're a photographer as well as a gardener, you can make good use of the airtight containers in which 35mm rolls of film are sold. A film processing lab might give you all you need.

When you have leftover seeds, take them out of the original package on a day when the humidity is low and seal them in the 35mm film cans. You don't want to get moisture in the cans, as it might cause the seeds to mold. Write the variety of seeds and the date on the can.

Small plastic bags are good for storing seeds, too. Paper bags tend to collect moisture. Put all the individual plastic bags in a coffee can or similar container and store on a closet shelf or in a cool, dry storage area. It's not cold but heat that destroys germination. In the spring, use the paper-towel test (see p.39) to determine the rate of germination.

CHAPTER 5
STARTING
PLANTS EARLY

MANY EXPERIENCED gardeners like to start some of their garden plants inside the house. There are at least three good reasons to start your own plants: starting varieties or types of plants that are not available as transplants, saving money by starting a lot of plants for a big or cash-crop garden, and making yourself feel that spring is just around the corner. Nothing feels more like spring than a few dozen seedlings on a sunny windowsill. And starting your own plants lets you stretch the gardening season by being ready to plant on your schedule rather than waiting for commercial transplants to arrive at the garden center.

A first-year gardener might want to experiment with growing a few plants indoors, but should not rely completely on homegrown plants. There is nothing wrong with buying a few things from the local garden center. In fact, in recent years the garden industry has learned that people don't have the time to start their plants indoors. As a result, more and more types of transplants are available in most areas.

A transplant is simply a plant started indoors well before the last frost date. It is set out into the garden well after the danger of frost is past. This gives it a head start and a long period of production before the season ends in the fall.

For starting plants inside, it is important to have either a good, sunny window with a southern exposure or some cool-white fluorescent bulbs. Keep heaters and heating ducts in mind as you select a place to start your plants. If there is a heater directly under your seed-starting window, your seedlings will dry out very quickly, and you will have to water them quite often.

There are all kinds of seed-starting containers for sale: peat pots; Jiffy Sevens, little cubes complete with soil; and seed flats. You can also use tin cans, milk cartons, and egg boxes. A lot of people use cardboard egg boxes, but I find that they absorb a lot of water, which causes plants to dry out too quickly. The egg boxes that work best are the ones made of Styrofoam or "dyefoam," and this is an excel-

STARTING SEEDS INDOORS

A soilless sterile mix, available at garden centers, is a good material in which to start seeds indoors. Dump some into a pail and moisten it thoroughly.

Fill containers to within 1 inch of the top and press the soil in firmly. A small piece of shingle or cardboard is a handy tool for tamping down soil. Sprinkle seeds across the soil and tamp them into place, then cover with soil to a depth of four times the seeds' diameter. Firm again. Cover the seeds with plastic and set them in a warm place out of direct sunlight.

Check the containers frequently. When the seeds germinate, remove the plastic and set them in a sunny spot.

lent way to recycle these containers. Try cutting the cover off and setting the bottom part of the box inside the cover. This double reinforcement will help make the box more sturdy.

Any container used for starting seeds must have holes in the bottom to allow excess water to escape. Most purchased pots and flats already have them. Peat pots, being very absorbent, drain readily, even without holes. Poke a dozen holes in an egg container with something sharp, like a nail. If you're using a large container, like a half-gallon milk carton, make some holes in the bottom, then put in about half an inch of gravel or crushed stone before you add soil.

Building Your Indoor Nursery

Fill your containers, preferably with a soilless mix such as Pro-Mix. These are sterile mixes you can buy at a garden center. Or you can make a batch of starter mixture. I recommend buying a good soilless mix. This is a dry mixture of peat moss and other ingredients. Be sure to moisten it thoroughly in a pail or other container before using it.

A sterile soilless mix prevents a common problem you run into when starting seeds indoors: damping-off. Damping-off is a fungal disease that occurs after seedlings are up an inch or two. Suddenly they just wither and fall over. The plant has been attacked by organisms in common soil. Soil can be sterilized by heating it in your oven, but it is a smelly process. Prevent the problem by using a soilless mix. You don't need to add fertilizer at planting time with soilless mixes, although I usually sprinkle 2 tablespoons of organic fertilizer per square foot at the very bottom of the container I plant in. Don't let it come in contact with the seeds, however.

Fill your containers almost to the top with the moistened mix. Level off the soil before you sprinkle any seeds on it. If you are using seed flats, a little piece of shingle works fine for leveling. Scrape over the top to make sure the soil mixture is even and smooth, then plant the seed.

If you are going to plant the seeds in rows, use the edge of the shingle to make ¼-inch troughs in the soil. Otherwise, spread the seed over the soil, evenly and not too thickly, then press them in with the flat side of the shingle. Cover them, remembering that they should be buried only to a depth of about four times their own diameter. Obviously, very fine seeds will require very shallow covering. Try to make sure that you spread an equal amount of soil over the whole area. Use the shingle to firm the soil a second time.

Newly planted seeds should be watered liberally but gently—preferably with a fine spray that will not disturb them. Next, the flats or pots should be put in plastic bags or covered with plastic to seal in moisture. You should not have to do any more watering until the seedlings come up. Put them in a place where the temperature remains in the neighborhood of 70° to 75°F. (about 21° to 24°C.).

Do not put them on a sunny windowsill yet. That's the worst place to put seeds before they germinate. It's the hottest place during the day and the coldest at night. Right now these seeds like a nice, warm, even temperature. The top of your refrigerator is perfect, if it's available. The higher up in the room the better, because the floor is the coldest place.

Germinating seeds do not require any light. In fact, if the flats are left in a very bright place, you might want to shade them with a piece of newspaper. Once the seeds begin to come up, remove the plastic immediately and place the

TESTING SEED GERMINATION

1. Spread ten seeds on a wet paper towel.

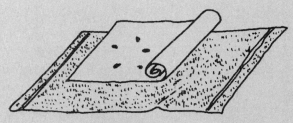

2. Roll up the seeds in the paper towel. Place the rolled paper towel on a soaked terrycloth face towel and roll that up.

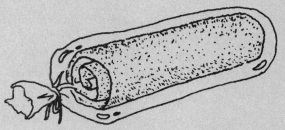

3. Put both rolled towels in a plastic bag and seal it.

4. In four to ten days, when the seeds have had time to sprout, carefully unwrap the towels and count the number of seeds that have germinated. If, for example, eight of the ten seeds have sprouted, the germination rate is 80 percent.

flat in a sunny window or under fluorescent lights. If your window has a heater under it, be careful not to dry out the transplants. A place in front of sliding glass doors is ideal for transplants. From this point on, you will have to water your plants regularly, as often as once a day if they are near a heater.

After they have been up for about a week it's time for a little fertilizer. The best way is to add an organic fertilizer to the water. Follow directions, because too much fertilizer is worse for your transplants, not better. It can force their growth and make them spindly.

Give Your Seedlings Room to Grow

The first leaves to push through the soil are not true leaves. They will be oval and smooth on the edges (spinach looks like this, even as a mature plant). True leaves are jagged and miniature versions of the grown plant. When three or four true leaves appear it's time to move most—but not all—of the tiny plants to deeper containers. They will be anywhere from 1 to 3 inches tall at this point and will probably be growing too close together. The seedlings should be transplanted a little deeper than they were before.

I used to transplant tomatoes like any other seedlings, but now I have a little trick to save me that effort. When I start tomatoes I only fill the container one-third full and leave 4 inches between the seeds. As they grow I add more soil mix around them. Tomatoes will form new roots where they contact the soil.

This trick is just like transplanting and works just as well for tomatoes, and it saves a lot of time. You'll be surprised at how well they do. If you do transplant tomatoes into new containers, make sure you plant them deeper. You can pick off the bottom two leaves and transplant them to just below the next set of leaves. All that stem will form a strong root system in tomatoes.

Don't add fertilizer at transplanting time. Don't replant peppers or cabbages more than an inch deeper than they were in the flat or you will risk smothering them. Transplanting sets a plant back a bit, stopping its upward growth and encouraging it to grow outward as it establishes a stronger root system. Every time you transplant, the seedling's root system will increase in size, sometimes even doubling. This enables the plant to pick up more nutrients from the soil and to better support itself as it grows.

It is a good idea to transplant whenever a plant starts to get leggy, or too elongated. Transplanting will set it back a bit and make the plant grow out instead of up. If I start early enough, I sometimes transplant seedlings three or four times.

Now is the time to add some sort of fertilizer: compost, manure, or a complete chemical fertilizer containing all three major nutrients—nitrogen, phosphorus, and potassium. Many potting compounds just provide a neutral growing medium, so it is up to you to feed the plants. If you have used soil from your garden, it can probably use a little shot of fertilizer, even if it is naturally rich.

SETTING OUT PEAT POTS

When planting peat pots, be sure they're thoroughly soaked. Tear off the bottom to encourage the roots to grow.

Homegrown Onions from Seed

Try growing some of your own onion plants from seed. Get a 4- or 5-inch-deep container with holes in the bottom, and put in some gravel or crushed stone. Fill it to within 1 inch of the top with a rich potting mixture and add a little fertilizer. Onion seeds need to be planted very early—12 or more weeks before you plan to set them out. I do this each year

THE OLD-FASHIONED WAY TO START SEEDS

1. When I was a youngster, we started seeds in blocks of sod cut from an out-of-the-way piece of lawn. These work well for plants that are hard to transplant like squash, pumpkins, and cucumbers. Using this method, you don't disturb the roots of the seedlings when you set them out.

2. These 2" x 2" "sod pots" were turned grass side down, placed in a container, and planted. Using treated seed reduces the likelihood of damping-off, but you should plant at least two or three seeds per block anyway, just to be on the safe side.

3. Give the seeded blocks a thorough watering.

4. Cover the container with plastic until the seeds germinate, then place them in a sunny window. You can transplant them directly into the garden after the last frost. The decomposing sod will provide nourishment for the new plants.

VEGETABLES SUITABLE FOR TRANSPLANTING AND METHODS OF SOWING SEED

Easy to Transplant. Can Be Sown in Flats in Rows and Transplanted Bare Root.

Broccoli	(5-7)
Brussels Sprouts	(5-7)
Cabbage	(5-7)
Cauliflower	(5-7)
Celeriac	(7-12)
Celery	(7-12)
Chinese Cabbage	(5-7)
Collards	(5-7)
*Eggplant	(6-8)
Lettuce	(5-7)
Onion	(12)
Parsley	(8-10)
*Peppers	(6-8)
Sweet Potato	(3-4) (start from tuber and not seed)
*Tomato	(6-8)

Must Be Started in Individual Containers and Transplanted without Disturbing Roots.

Cantaloupe	(3-4)
All Muskmelons	(3-4)
Cucumbers	(3-4)
Squash	(3-4) (summer & winter varieties)
Watermelon	(5-7)

* Sometimes sown in flats and then transplanted into individual containers before transplanting to garden.

( ) Number in parentheses is approximate time (weeks) from sowing seed to transplanting to garden.

Many vegetables like corn, beans, and beets can be started early in pots and flats, but seldom are because the large number of pots needed is impractical.

with Bermuda onions, and I have had great success.

The thing to remember about onions is that the tops may grow quite leggy because they have no leaves to absorb the sun. When the tops get to be somewhere between 3 and 4 inches tall, they need to be cut back to a height of about an inch and a half. Then, every other week or so—whenever they get 3 or 4 inches tall again—cut them back. You will have to do this continuously until it is time to set the plants outside to harden off. With onions, we are naturally interested in the bottoms. Every time the tops are cut off, the plant's energy goes into growing a larger root. Don't bother to transplant onions inside. Plant them once, keep them cut, and when the time is right, harden them off and transplant outside.

Save Money with Sod

Here is a good trick that you can use with hard-to-transplant vegetables such as cucumbers and melons. Cut a thick piece of sod out of a field, turn it bottom-side-up with the grassy side down, and cut it into pieces about 2 inches square. Plant a seed or two in each of these pieces. After the seed has germinated and the plant has grown a bit, transplant it, sod and all, into a pot or into the garden. This way, the plant's tender roots will not be disturbed at all. The soil in sod is apt to be quite rich, and as the grass decomposes in the pot or in the ground, nutrients for the plant will be released. This is a good way, incidentally, to avoid buying expensive peat pots.

Cucumbers and melons can be started in either pots or sod, but they should not be planted until two or three weeks before the last frost. Otherwise, they will get too tall and may not survive the transplant.

Prepare Your Sheltered Seedlings for a Shock

Plants are just like people in some ways. They eat, breathe, drink, windburn, sunburn, catch cold, and suffer from stress. Have you ever noticed how easy it is to get a sunburn or windburn in the early spring? Because you have spent most of the winter inside, your skin is not as accustomed to the weather as it would be, say, in August. Plants can be just as tender as you are in this respect. They have been sitting on your windowsill or in a cold frame for weeks. If you suddenly take them out into the bright sun, wind, and colder air they can really suffer.

When you first set them out in their containers, don't put them in the bright sun and hold off on water for the first day to encourage tough stems. Outdoors you may not have to water as often as you did inside the house, but keep an eye on your plants and don't let them get too dry. I set them in a shaded area for just a couple of hours the first day out. The next day I put them in the early morning sun for two or three hours. The third day, if it's sunny, I leave them out most of the day. It's very important to protect them from the wind or they will windburn or even die. They're very tender and can actually break off in the wind. I've seen tomato plants with leaves as thin and white as tracing paper because they weren't hardened off.

Remember, these plants have had tender loving care up until now and it might take a week or two for them to adjust to life outside. If the weather turns unusually hot or cold or windy you may want to move them in and out of the house several times before finally setting them into the garden.

Build a Quick and Easy "Plant Bank"

After years of trying many methods, I've found that the best way to start both flowers and vegetables is to do it in the mini outdoor greenhouses I call "plant banks." If you want just a small, very early garden you could plant the entire garden in a plant bank. Or use one to stretch the season in the fall. I like these "plant banks" because you can grow so much in them and get a real jump on the growing season.

For the very hardy plants that can stand a little frost—like lettuce, cabbage, cauliflower, broccoli, kale, flowering kale, chard, even beets—I start in early April as soon as I can work the ground. I don't start melons and cukes in the plant bank because they should be transplanted in the container in which they start. You could, though, start melons and cukes in peat pots in the plant bank. Just be careful not to let them dry out. Later in April, when it warms up, I plant tomatoes, peppers, eggplant—even okra.

SWEET POTATOES UP NORTH

You can buy a sweet potato or yam at the supermarket to grow your own. Simply slice it in half lengthwise and place the two halves in a pie tin of water with the eyes facing up. Set it on a shelf and sprouts will grow. It takes a long time, but you can then set the sprouts directly out in the garden 4 or 5 inches deep. Like a tomato, all the stem under the ground will form roots. Here in Vermont I've never had any luck growing them any other way. But you've never tasted a sweet potato until you've grown your own and served them fresh from the garden.

"Plant banks" can be made to any size. A 2" x 4" frame provides the anchor for plastic piping. I seed very heavily in my plant bank—a packet of seeds for every square foot.

Plant banks are very easy to use because you can start so many seedlings this way, and then just transplant each of them directly into the garden when the time is right for them to be set out. Just make a "withdrawal" from your plant bank.

Here's how to make a plant bank. You can make them almost any dimension, but 4' x 8' is a good size to start. The larger they are, the more heat they are able to store. First, rototill or spade the soil where your plant bank will be. Set the frame in place temporarily and mark the spot.

For each greenhouse you will need:

☼ Three 2" x 4" x 8' boards. Two boards make the sides and the third is cut in half for the ends.

☼ A length of ½- or ¾-inch black plastic water pipe. These form the bows or supports for the greenhouse. Mine are 10 feet long spaced about 3 feet apart, so I need four sections, or a 40-foot length. The pipe cuts easily with a saw. Drill ½- or ¾-inch holes in the 2" x 4"s where you want to place a support. For smaller ones, you can use a pipe to pound a hole in the ground and just push the ends of the hose into these starter holes.

Stretch a sheet of 4 to 8 mil clear plastic over the framework and hold the edges down with dirt or stones. Gather the plastic at the end together and use soil to hold it down, or tie it to a stake pounded into the ground.

Pick a nice warm day and prepare the soil by adding compost or organic fertilizer and working it into the soil to a depth of 4 or 5 inches. You'll need about a 5-gallon pail full of compost or 2 pounds of organic fertilizer. Before planting, it's a good idea to wait a day with the soil covered with clear plastic or with the greenhouse in place. If it's sunny, it will really warm it up. Then use a rake to level it off, just like planting a flat. Then mark it off into square feet.

I plant very heavily in the plant bank—a packet of seeds in every square foot of soil, even more with some tomato packets that don't have many seeds. So, in a 4' x 8' space I have 32 different varieties. I have a very big garden, so you can adapt what you plant to whatever you need. Try to put the taller plants to the north side of the plant bank, so they won't shade the smaller ones, and the hardier plants around the edge where it cools off sooner. If you're planting two or three varieties of the same vegetable—tomatoes, for example—it's easier to keep track of what you've planted if you don't plant them side by side. Either make a chart of what you've planted where, or put the seed packet in each square, mounted on a stick or piece of cardboard.

I cover the seeds with just a little bit of soil, and then a layer of soilless mix. It's at the surface that damping-off takes place, and a layer of soilless mix on top helps to prevent it. Use the back of a large hoe to firm the soil down to make sure the seeds have complete contact with the soil. If you use only soil, make sure there is a half inch of soil covering the seeds. Then water gently. You'll really have to soak the soil if you use the soilless mix. Stick your finger in to see how deep the water has penetrated. For good germination, the seeds must be moistened and not allowed to dry out.

Now cover the frame with the plastic and bury the edges with soil or stones.

Check the plant bank after three or four

Plastic piping provides the ribs for the plant bank. Clear plastic sheeting is stretched over it. A similar arrangement, using netting or screening instead of plastic, can be used to protect crops from birds, flying insects, or the hot sun.

The plastic can be pulled back as days grow warmer to "harden off" the plants and prepare them for transplanting into the garden. Some, like leaf lettuce, can be left in the plant bank permanently.

days to see if it needs watering, especially if you've been having warm weather. Don't let the seeds dry out. Water every few days, if necessary. Soon you'll be seeing things come up.

Once the plants have a good start you can open up the plant bank for a few hours on warm days. Cloudy days are better than sunny ones for the first few exposures, and you might want to leave the plastic draped over the north side to shelter the plants from the wind. Increase their exposed time, but cover them at night until about a week before you are ready to set them out. Watch out for a surprise late frost. Crops like broccoli, cauliflower, and kale will stand a frost and can even be set into the garden before the last frost, but other plants in the plant bank might not be so hardy. Don't add any fertilizer during this time in the plant bank.

Before transplanting, give the plants a thorough soaking. It's a good idea to have the garden prepared before you remove the plants from the plant bank—dig the hole and have the soil fertilized and watered. This will minimize the time the root systems of your transplants are exposed to the air. When you dig the transplants, take as much soil as you can so the roots are protected. A cloudy day is better for transplanting than a sunny one.

You'll have more than enough transplants for yourself and to share with all your friends. Your garden will get about a two-week head start. If you start lettuce, beets, and other crops you normally start from seed it's like having an instant garden. You should still start some from seed to stretch the harvest.

There are other things I like about these plant banks. One is that starting plants indoors takes up quite a bit of space, but that doesn't matter here. Plus, I can start some things that I normally wouldn't—like lettuce. It's amazing how quickly you'll get a crop. It's about the only way to get iceberg head lettuce like the kind we buy in the store.

CHAPTER 6

FINALLY
IT'S TIME TO PLANT!

PLANTING TIME is one of the most exciting and critical periods of the gardening season. Your crop will be abundant only if you plant carefully.

First, let's talk about setting out plants you've started early in your hotbed or bought at a garden center.

Taking a plant out of its container and placing it in the ground gives it a terrible shock. The best time to do this is in the late afternoon or evening if the day is sunny. A cloudy day would be better still.

Soak the flats thoroughly before you remove the plants. The soil should be pure mud. The muddier the potting soil, the less the roots will be exposed to the air as they are removed from the containers. Try to have your rows laid out, your furrows or holes dug, and your fertilizer applied, so that everything is ready before the actual transplanting takes place. Use your fingers or a spoon to take the plant out of its container. Keep as much mud around the roots as you can. Set the plant in the prepared furrow or hole immediately, cover the roots with soil, and firm it down thoroughly. Don't be afraid to water recently transplanted vegetables generously. It is nearly impossible to overwater when you are moving plants from pots to garden soil.

New transplants must be protected from wind and frost. If you use hotcaps to protect your transplants, you can steal some time from Mother Nature by transplanting a week or two before the average date of the last killing frost.

Check all purchased plants for bugs. Any plants raised in a greenhouse may have aphids, spiders, or whiteflies on them. These insects can do a lot of damage, so you will want to dust the plants with rotenone or some other insecticide before setting them out in the garden.

In the spring, there is always the danger of cutworms—small creatures that chew off plant stems flush with the top of the ground. Protecting your young plants against them is not much of a problem. Tear newspaper into pieces about 2 inches by 3 inches. Wrap one of these around each plant stem so that about half the paper shows above the soil and half is below.

I sprinkle radishes in the rows with almost everything I plant. They come up fast to mark the row. As I harvest them, they make room for their neighbors to grow.

The paper will last long enough to keep cutworms away during the critical early growing period. By the time the plant is strong enough to stand on its own, the newspaper collar will have rotted away.

Rules to Remember at Planting Time

1. Hardy vegetables can stand some shade and "wet feet" because they are cool-weather crops.

2. Root crops can tolerate some shade and damp (but not very wet) feet. The same is true of cabbage, broccoli, Brussels sprouts, and cauliflower.

3. Vine crops, like cucumbers, melons, and squash, as well as tomatoes, peppers, corn, eggplant, and beans, all require a lot of sunshine and dry feet.

Wide-Row Planting

There are two ways to plant—in single rows or in wide rows. Single-row planting means that you make an indentation in the soil—a furrow or a small trench—and plant your seeds in a single line. If you plant in wide rows, on the other hand, you use two lengths of string to mark off a row which is about 16 inches wide, or about the width of a normal steel rake. I use this width because I don't like to rake the whole garden; I rake only where I am going to plant, the area between the two strings. I find that if I rake the whole garden area, I tread the soil down with my feet too much, making it very hard and compact. Packed-down soil does not make a good seedbed. I make no indentations at all between the strings. I simply level and smooth the soil with my rake. It always helps to work from the same side of a row. This way the soil between rows stays looser.

Now I am ready to plant. Take lettuce, for example. I broadcast the seed over the area between the strings. You should do this in much the same way that you would seed a lawn. Just remember to spread the seed somewhat thinner than grass seed.

After I have planted lettuce seed, I sprinkle a few radish seeds in the same row. This serves two purposes:

1. The radishes will come up in three or four days—much earlier than the lettuce. They will mark the rows and can be harvested long before the lettuce is ready.

2. When the radishes are pulled, the row will automatically be thinned and cultivated. Each time a radish is pulled out, a little cavity is left in the soil. The roots of the other plants can then grow into the loose soil around the cavity.

If you have heavy clay soil and want to raise carrots, beets, or other root crops, try planting icicle radishes along with them. I don't harvest them to eat; I wait until they get about

HOW TO PLANT A WIDE ROW

1. The first step for any kind of seed planting is to turn the soil over, break up any lumps, and even it out with a rake. Then you can make a wide row as I'm doing here. Stake out the row according to your garden plan. Mark it by pulling a rake along the string. A rake's width is good for a wide row.

2. Place the seeds in the row. Large seeds, like peas and beans, can be spaced as you plant. Small seeds, like carrots, should be sprinkled evenly over the bed and thinned later with a rake after the plants appear. I often plant radishes with other seeds in a wide row because they come up in about a week and mark the row.

3. Tamp the uncovered seeds down with the back of a hoe to make sure that they are in firm contact with the soil.

4. Using a garden rake, reach across the row and pull soil over the wide row to cover the seeds. A good rule of thumb is to cover seeds with soil to a depth of four times their diameter.

5. Using the back of the hoe again, tamp the soil down around the seeds to make sure they are in firm contact with the soil. Water them thoroughly but gently. Soon you'll see a productive row of plants come up that will form a living mulch to shade out weeds and hold in moisture.

SPACING ROWS FAR APART

Planting long vine crops such as watermelons and pumpkins closer than recommended will make working them easier. Space them 12 to 18 inches apart in hills in the row instead of the normal 6 to 8 feet. But make the rows 10 to 12 feet apart to give the vines plenty of room to spread out.

You can plant a fast-maturing crop like radishes or lettuce between the rows, harvest them, and till the remains before the vines reach the middles.

twice as big as my thumb and then pull them. Because they are long, they leave a deep cavity in the soil. As the beets and carrots ex-

pand, they can fill up the "shoulder room" left by the radishes.

Radishes can be planted with many different crops. One morning before I went to work, I started pulling radishes out of my spinach. I noticed that many of the radish leaves had been eaten by insects, but that the spinach leaves had hardly been touched. It isn't that radishes keep bugs away from spinach. Bugs just like radishes better.

Don't Let Plants Get Too Close for Comfort

Vegetable plants that grow too close together will be stunted and sickly. They need elbow room. It is hard to pull up little plants that are growing well, but it needs to be done. Spacing plants properly by removing others is called *thinning*. How do we thin? I use an iron rake with stiff teeth to do my first thinning. I drag it slowly across the wide row, digging in about ¼ inch and taking out a good share of the plants. I try to do this when the plants are anywhere from ½ inch to 1 inch high. I do this first thinning in both single-row and wide-row plantings.

You don't have to thin peas or beans; the seeds are larger, so it is fairly easy to control how closely you plant them. Small, finer seeds are harder to space because they roll off your hand so fast as you plant them.

The second thinning is the pulling of the radishes described above. The third thinning takes place when you begin harvesting. You can make the first fresh salad of the season with thinnings from your lettuce patch. Thin by pulling the biggest, most edible plants. The smaller ones will grow to replace the ones you remove. Keep doing this until the spacing is about right.

You can do the same thing with carrots. When they are about the size of your little finger, they make good eating. This is when they are really succulent. It is easy to select the largest ones; they are almost always the ones with the largest, darkest green leaves.

Vegetables That Can Be Grown in Wide Rows

Here is a list of crops that I like to plant in wide rows: carrots; beets; lettuce; dill; chard, spinach, collards, and all other greens; onions, both from seed and from sets; Chinese cabbage; rutabagas; turnips; beans; and especially peas.

Carrots and Beets—These root crops are slow in coming up. Icicle radishes mark rows early and do a good job of cultivating when they are pulled.

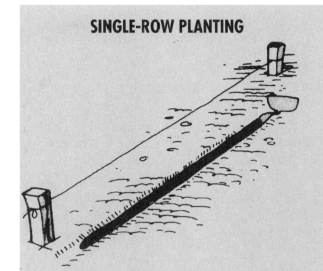

SINGLE-ROW PLANTING

1. Rake Smooth
Rake over the area to be planted. A smooth seedbed is particularly important with very fine seeds.

2. Stake and Make Row
Drive a stake at each end of the row and stretch a string between them. To make a furrow, lay your hoe directly under the string and step on it. Repeat down the length of the row.

3. Drop Seed
Drop seeds into the row, spacing them correctly. (See chart on pages 176-183.)

4. Cover with Soil
Firm the soil by walking down the row or by tamping with a hoe or a rake.

Onion Sets and Seeds—These are easy to plant. Grip each bulb by the top (the pointed end) and push it into the soil. In a row that is 16 inches wide, you can plant six or seven onion sets side by side, move down the row 2 or 3 inches, plant another six or seven, and so on. There is no need to make any sort of trench in

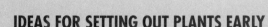

IDEAS FOR SETTING OUT PLANTS EARLY

Put a "Soldier's Hat" over Plants for Frost Protection

Remember as a kid making a play soldier's hat to march around in? Now you can put such hats to good use. Take a newspaper and fold it in half. Take the two upper corners and fold them so that they meet at the exact center. Now fold the bottom flaps up, one on each side. Open the hat out and place it over young plants when frost threatens, held down with small stones or dirt at each end.

Hotcaps are wax-paper cones placed over individual plants to protect them from frost and wind. Hotcaps cost a dime apiece or less, depending on the quantity bought. You can save money by using paper "soldier's hats," old boxes, fruit baskets, or plastic jugs with the bottoms cut out instead of hotcaps.

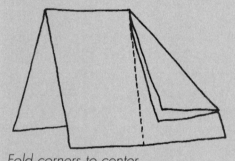

Fold corners to center

Fold bottom flaps up

Hotcap

Cardboard box

Plastic jug

---

the soil. Pushing the bulbs in with your fingers works fine.

Lettuce, looseleaf or head—A good rule of thumb for planting any seed is that its depth be three or four times the diameter of the seed itself. So lettuce seed should be covered with a very small amount of soil. Then gently tamp down the seedbed so the seeds will have good contact with the soil. This also shuts out air and protects tender sprouts from drying out.

Peas—The only way I know to get a decent crop of peas is to plant them in a wide row. A rake-width row may not be broad enough. In fact, I have often used rows 4 feet wide. I simply broadcast the seed in wide bands and then walk on the soil. Next, I turn the rake upside down and drag it back and forth over my footprints. Occasionally, I reach over to the side and pull a little extra dirt over onto the seeds. It doesn't take much; walking on the seeds usually pushes them far enough into the soil. This is especially true if the soil has been carefully prepared for planting and has what we call good "tilth."

Beans —You can grow a tremendous crop of snap beans in a wide row. I usually plant them in rows that are 10 inches wide. I plant three or four beans across the row, move down the row to plant another two or three, and so on. The main advantage to this method is that you can produce four, five, even six times as many beans as in a single row because you don't have so much walk area, which is actually wasted growing space. I sometimes plant beans in rows as wide as 3 or 4 feet.

Wide-row planting has an advantage when you are weeding, too. When you weed a single row, you can reach only about 3 feet of row from one position. If you have a 3-foot-wide row, which is equivalent to five or six single rows, you can figure that each time you weed 3 feet down the row, you are weeding a space which is equivalent to 9 to 15 feet of single row! The same proves true at harvest time. Each time you stoop down beside the wide row, you can reach a 3-foot area. But in that 3-foot area, you can probably pick a peck of produce without having to move!

Wide-row planting really works. The average gardener, using the single-row method, might plant a 20-foot row of lettuce. If he or she plants a row 10 inches wide instead, there will be enough in 20 feet to equal 100 feet the old way. A family of four needs only about 6 feet of lettuce planted in a wide row. Try putting in 3 feet of one variety and 3 feet of another. You won't be able to keep ahead of it all! In the rest of the row, you might plant beets, chard, or carrots.

There is still another advantage. We know that weeds don't grow well on shaded ground. When you plant crops in wide rows, you automatically shade the ground. Very few weeds, if any, will do well within the rows—with the exception of a few grasses which grow tall and are easy to pull. Most weeds will be smothered out. This is what I call a "shade mulch" because the leaves of the plants themselves shade the soil. This saves many hours of backbreaking weeding.

Experiment with wide rows this year. You can grow four to five times more produce than you can grow in single rows using the same amount of space. It makes thinning, weeding, and harvesting simpler because the whole area is laid out right in front of you—within easy reach.

CHAPTER 7
FERTILIZING
FOR HUNGRY PLANTS

WHAT IS FERTILIZER and what does it do for the garden? In garden supply stores, you've probably seen bags of fertilizer with three numbers on them. They might read 5–10–5, 10–10–10, or 5–10–10. There might even be a fourth number, so that the bag reads 5–10–10–2. What does all this mumbo-jumbo mean?

There are three things—besides soil, water, air, and sunlight—that plants need to grow and produce fruit. We call these three things major nutrients. They are nitrogen (N), phosphorus (P), and potassium (K), which is sometimes called potash. The home gardener with average soil needs a fertilizer that contains at least these three elements. The numbers on the fertilizer bag describe the percentages of N, P, and K inside. So, 5–10–10 contains 5 percent nitrogen, 10 percent phosphorus, and 10 percent potassium.

Nitrogen (N) is essential to all growing vegetation. It gives a plant its healthy, dark green color. A plant that lacks nitrogen is apt to look yellow and sickly. When nitrogen is added to the soil, plants may suddenly put on tremendous growth. We have to be careful, though, not to provide too much nitrogen, because if a plant grows too fast—getting quite high and putting out a lot of leaves—the fruit will not be so good. Chemical fertilizers can also actually burn plants. What we are looking for is healthy growth, not overgrowth.

Phosphorus (P) is the major nutrient that helps plants grow strong roots. It is especially important for root crops like carrots, beets, potatoes, and turnips.

Potassium or potash (K) helps to condition the whole plant. It helps it grow and bear fruit and makes it resistant to disease.

Organic vs. Chemical Fertilizers—The Choice Is Yours

Before the early 19th century, the major fertilizers used by expert gardeners were *humus*—vegetable matter in its final form of decomposition—and manure.

But scientists of the day proclaimed that soil was simply chemistry—in other words, NPK—and they could analyze soil to prove it. Chemical fertilizers were seen as the quick-fix solution for poor soil, and the appeal of that notion launched a chain of events that continues even today. Lost in the shuffle was the fact that science was at that time unable to detect bacteria in the soil. Chemicals do work, at least in the short run, and the fact that soil is a living thing is easy to forget when the life-forms are too tiny to see.

Some time in the future we will learn whether or not we have traded our true wealth—resources like the soil—for money. Like a foolish heir, perhaps we are squandering the principal instead of living well on the interest. Some Caribbean islands, like Haiti, have already learned the consequences of that. We all just happen to share a larger island.

Organic fertilizers are quite different from chemical fertilizers, even though nitrates and phosphates are found in nature and are mined to be included in chemical fertilizers.

1. Organic fertilizers not only feed the plant; they also feed the soil, which is hungry in its own way. Overuse of chemical fertilizers can actually harm soil life.
2. Organic fertilizers are less concentrated. You may see a 5–3–4 or 3–2–2 organic. By comparison, you can buy concentrated water-soluble chemical fertilizers, often used on houseplants, that are 15–30–15.
3. Chemical fertilizers tend to be more

A variety of natural fertilizers is available at most garden centers. Dried blood, bonemeal, and cottonseed meal are among them.

water-soluble than organic fertilizers and leach out of the soil faster, delivering much less bang for the buck than you might think. As much as 50 percent of the chemical fertilizer can leach out before the plant can use it. Organic fertilizers become part of the soil.

4. Chemical fertilizers pack a wallop directly to the plant. As a result, it is possible to overfertilize and use chemicals counterproductively. Usually this shows up as fertilizer burn or a massive amount of plant foliage with little crop production. Organic fertilizers work with the soil to release beneficial trace nutrients, and they work very gradually to release all nutrients as the plant needs them.
5. Application of an organic fertilizer at planting time reduces the need for additional applications during the season, while side-dressing with chemicals at about the time most plants blossom is recommended. Heavy feeders, like onions, and crops with a long growing season (tomatoes, corn,

When using commercial fertilizer like these granules, your plants should be "spoon-fed" just as they set blossoms. One tablespoon in a trench around the plant will be enough. Make sure you cover it with soil to prevent the fertilizer from splashing up and burning the plants. Compost and other organic fertilizers will not burn plants, but cover them up, too, to put them to work faster and to keep them from washing away.

and peppers, for example) will benefit from organic fertilizers that are worked into the soil around them and then watered in.
6. A wide variety of materials found in nature can be used as organic fertilizers. Chemical fertilizers usually come concentrated as granules or in liquid form.

Most of the materials I recommended putting into your compost pile double as both organic matter and fertilizer (see page 28).

Over the years I have used all kinds of fertilizers, including chemicals. You can choose one or the other, or both. Some gardeners choose to be "morganic"—more organic than chemical, but still using some chemicals. In this chapter you'll find information on both. Another section in this book deals with "green manures" (see page 168).

Avoid Using Too Much of a Good Thing

Every home gardener should be careful with commercial chemical fertilizers. Some of the worst gardening failures are the result of adding too much fertilizer. A person might say to himself, "That little handful of fertilizer I used helped me so much last year, I think I'll use *two* handfuls this year." Two disastrous things could happen as a result of this kind of thinking. The plants could be seriously burned and killed by the chemicals in the fertilizer, or the plants could grow large but produce little or no fruit at all.

I use a very simple formula for spreading chemical fertilizer. One day before planting, I fill a 12-quart pail with 5–10–10 or 10–10–10 fertilizer and broadcast it over 1,000 square feet of garden space. The fertilizer should be mixed—either with a tiller or by hand—into the top 2 or 3 inches of soil. This should be all the fertilizer you need to get plants started. Spreading fertilizer over a broad area like this is safer than putting it down in rows.

Later on, I apply a *side-dressing*—an additional bit of fertilizer that is put into the soil not far from the roots of the plants themselves. If you use this method, you can control the amount of fertilizer that is going into your garden and still give individual crops a boost as

PRIMARY PLANT FOOD ELEMENTS

Element	Symbol	Function in Plant	Deficiency Symptoms	Excess Symptoms	Sources
NITROGEN	N	Gives dark green color to plant. Increases growth of leaf and stem. Influences crispness and quality of leaf crops. Stimulates rapid early growth.	Light green to yellow leaves. Stunted growth.	Dark green, excessive growth. Retarded maturity. Loss of buds or fruit.	Urea, Ammonia Nitrates
PHOSPHORUS	P	Stimulates early formation and growth of roots. Gives plants a rapid and vigorous start. Is important in formation of seed. Gives hardiness to fall-seeded grasses and grains.	Red or purple leaves. Cell division retardation.	Possible tie-up of other essential elements.	Super-phosphate, Rock phosphate
POTASH	K	Increases vigor of plants and resistance to disease. Stimulates production of strong, stiff stalks. Promotes production of sugar, starches, oils. Increases plumpness of grains and seed. Improves quality of crop yield.	Reduced vigor. Susceptibility to diseases. Thin skin and small fruit.	Coarse, poor colored fruit. Reduced absorption of calcium and magnesium.	Muriate or Sulphate of Potash

they need it.

All garden plants benefit from a side-dressing just as they begin to blossom. The fertilizer will help the vegetable or fruit to fill out. Vegetables will sometimes let you know when it is time for that extra bit of fertilizer. The cucumber, for example, will stand up and start to blossom just before it lays its vines down along the ground. This brief standing period gives you a chance to reach within 3 or 4 inches of the stem so you can get fertilizer right to the roots. Some types of squash will do the same thing.

Organic matter can add many nutrients on its own, and by using it, you can reduce the need for fertilizer.

PHOSPHATE IN OLD GARDENS

If a plot has been farmed or gardened for many years, chances are the soil has a reserve supply of phosphate, which is long-lasting in the soil. This means you can use a fertilizer that is higher in nitrogen and potash and save money by adding less phosphate. When planting, it is good to use a complete, balanced fertilizer to insure the development of a good root system. The plant needs the roots in order to pick up the reserve phosphate.

RECOMMENDED TIMES FOR SIDE-DRESSING VEGETABLES

Crop	Time of Application
Asparagus	Before growth starts in spring, and after harvesting to promote fern growth.
*Beans	No need to side-dress
*Beets	No need to side-dress
Broccoli	Three weeks after transplanting
Cabbage	Three weeks after transplanting
*Carrots	No need to side-dress
Cauliflower	Three weeks after transplanting
Cucumbers	At "stand up" stage just before they start to run
Eggplant	When plants start to blossom
Kale	Four weeks after planting
*Lettuce	No need to side-dress
Muskmelon	At "stand up" stage, just before plants start to run
Onions	Four weeks and six weeks after planting
*Peas	No need to side-dress
Peppers	When plants start to blossom
Potatoes	At last hilling, before plants start to blossom
*Spinach	No need to side-dress
Squash	At "stand up" stage, just before plants start to run
Tomatoes	When plants start to blossom
*Turnips	No need to side-dress
Watermelon	At "stand up" stage, just before plants start to run

*Assuming fertilizer has been added to the rows before planting.

New Life for Old Gardens

As people get more and more interested in gardening these days, old, forgotten garden plots are being put to use again. A simple rule of thumb seems to work well for a new garden or for one which has lain fallow for four or five years. Add plenty of organic matter and test the soil's pH. Add organic fertilizer at planting time.

This is one important value of organic and natural plant foods. They usually supply a num-

PLANT FOOD ELEMENTS

In 1840 the soil scientist Leibig stated his law of the minimum which goes as follows: "Crop yields are determined by the quantity of the element that is present in the least abundance."

This means that a plant will not grow properly if the soil is low in one particular element. No matter how much nitrogen you might pour on, if the soil is deficient in magnesium, it still won't show a rich natural green color.

Leibig's law can be illustrated by picturing a barrel in your mind. If one stave of the barrel is short, the water in the barrel can't rise any higher than the shortest stave.

On some soils, it is especially important to recognize this point. The soil might be rich in all the major food elements, but a deficiency in a minor trace element will stunt the plants. You can guess and add all kinds of fertilizers by trial and error, but it won't do any good until the soil is brought into balance with the missing plant food element.

ber of trace elements along with the major nutrients nitrogen, phosphorus, and potash.

The chart at right will help you to adapt fertilizer recommendations for large acreages to a small garden.

For small amounts of fertilizer it is easier to measure by volume than by weight. To convert charts that call for pounds you can figure that 1 pound of common garden fertilizer is equivalent to 2 cupfuls.

Some Organic Substitutes for Chemical Fertilizers

Most commercial fertilizers are made with chemicals. But there are other kinds of fertilizer, and they do not come in a bag from a garden supply store. I mean natural, organic fertilizers. They are easy to find and are usually cheap, sometimes free. I am talking about manures, compost, soybean and cottonseed meal, seaweed, decomposed hay and straw, crop residues, leaves, and grass clippings. When you mulch with these materials, you are adding fertilizer to your garden.

Cow manure is one of the most common manures, but horse manure, rabbit manure, chicken manure, duck manure, sheep manure, and goat manure are sometimes available too. Some manures are very strong. Cow manure, for instance, should be aged before it is put on the garden. It should be piled up outside for three to six months. If you can't wait this long, spread fresh manure over the garden a couple of weeks before planting, and then mix it into the top 2 or 3 inches of soil very, very thoroughly—either with a tiller or with a plow and harrow. It's best not to use fresh manure in a row or as a side-dressing. If you do, you are likely to burn your seeds or injure your plants. Fresh manure has a very high percentage of

RATES OF APPLICATION OF DIFFERENT FERTILIZER FORMULAS

(as recommended for 1,000 square feet or for a 10-foot wide or single row)

Fertilizer Formula	1,000 sq.ft.	10 ft. Single Row	10 ft. Wide Row
5-10-5	40 lbs.	2 cups	6 cups
8-32-16	25 lbs.	1½ cups	4½ cups
10-6-4	20 lbs.	1 cup	3 cups
12-12-12	17 lbs.	1 cup	3 cups

TRACE ELEMENTS

Chemical analysis shows that a plant may contain as many as 40 elements; however, only 15 are necessary to its normal functioning. Three elements—carbon, oxygen, and hydrogen—account for about 90 percent of the dry weight of an average plant. Nitrogen, phosphate, and potash are the primary plant foods found in all complete commercial fertilizers. Though they occur in much smaller quantities than the three essential elements (nitrogen is only 1.5 percent of total dry plant weight), the primary plant foods have tremendous effect on growth and general health. The secondary plant foods (magnesium, manganese, copper, zinc, iron, sulfur, calcium, and molybdenum) occur in even more minute quantities, but they too are very important. For example, a lack of iron, which acts as a catalyst in the enzyme system, causes leaves to turn yellow except for the veins, which stay green. If you suspect your soil of being deficient in elements which don't show up on ordinary soil tests, you might want to send a sample to the Extension Service at your state university.

Dehydrated and composted manures and organic fertilizers are becoming more available as demand for them increases.

ORGANIC SOIL BUILDING: A CASE STUDY

Donald Roberts of Kilmarnock, Virginia, hauls in crab shells when they are available from commercial watermen and spreads them on his garden. The shells contain lime and many trace minerals that would be expensive to buy in a bag. He spreads anything on his garden that rots—leaves, straw, manure, and all his garbage and grass clippings.

Under his corn one year, he put 20 bushels of frozen fish that had gone bad in a freezing locker. He opened up a furrow, spread the fish down the row, covered it over and planted his corn. He needed very little commercial fertilizer and had a bumper crop.

At planting time, Mr. Roberts opens up a double row with his plow, fills the furrow with plenty of cow manure and throws the dirt back over it. That's what he plants his tomatoes, cucumbers, squash, and eggplant on. They take off fast and don't know when to quit growing.

water, so a bushel of aged and dried manure contains more organic matter and more nutrients than a bushel of fresh manure.

Cow manure is available to more people than any other kind. You can use quite a bit of it without worrying about overfertilizing.

I like to put aged cow manure in the bottom of a furrow and plant seeds on top of it. The only drawback is that cow manure contains some weed seeds. Whenever you broadcast it over the entire garden, you are making work for yourself by planting some extra weeds. But I have found that putting it in furrows virtually eliminates this problem, possibly because the weed seeds are buried too deep to germinate successfully.

Chicken manure is very high in nitrogen. Use it very sparingly. If you use too much, it will either burn your plants or make them grow huge tops with few good vegetables. Chicken manure from poultry farms is usually mixed with sawdust or wood chips, and this dilutes the potency of the manure. Even so, the safest way to use it is to sprinkle it lightly over the soil and work it in.

There is no danger of burning your plants when you till old hay, grass, leaves, and similar organic substances into the soil. In fact, it is impossible to use too much of these things. They will use up some nitrogen in the soil for a while as they continue to decay, but this debt will be repaid as soon as the microorganisms have had a chance to do their work.

Compost is a wonderful fertilizer, although it varies in strength depending on the ingredients put into it. Most plants will thrive in compost. It may be all the fertilizer they need. For a more in-depth discussion of compost, see Chapter 3.

A garden which has been fertilized only with manures, compost, or organic matter will probably show a lack of phosphorus before too long. A light application of rock phosphate, an organic fertilizer, or a sprinkling of superphosphate, a chemical fertilizer, will be helpful from time to time. On the other hand, if you are careful about making compost from a wide range of different things, you may be produc-

"I plant lettuce along with the turnip greens and broccoli about the end of September. The cold-hardy turnip tops protect the more tender lettuce from the frost. Our winters are mild enough that I have small lettuce plants among the turnips to transplant in early spring." DR

MAGNESIUM IN THE SOIL

"I've grown beans on the same land for 30 years. But one year my beans began to die. I had a complete soil test done and found I needed the trace element magnesium. I added this element by applying Epsom salts, and the problem was corrected immediately. The state university soil test, which I use every year, doesn't break the soil needs down far enough to recognize the lack of these trace elements." JLG

APPROXIMATE COMPOSITION OF NATURAL FERTILIZER MATERIALS

Material	Nitrogen (N)	Phosphoric Acid (P)	Potash (K)
Bulky Organic Materials			
Alfalfa hay or meal	2.5	0.5	2.0
Grain straw	0.6	0.2	1.0
Oak leaves	0.8	0.4	0.02
Peanut hulls	1.5	-	0.8
Seaweed (kelp)	1.7	0.8	5.0
Timothy hay	1.0	0.2	1.5
Winery pomaces	1.5	1.5	0.8
Manures			
Cow manure, dried	1.3	0.9	0.8
Cow manure, fresh	0.5	0.2	0.5
Hen manure, dried, with litter	5.0	2.8	1.5
Horse manure, fresh	0.6	0.3	0.5
Pig manure, fresh	0.6	0.5	0.4
Sheep manure, dried	1.4	1.0	3.0
Sheep manure, fresh	0.9	0.5	0.8
Rock Powders			
Basic slag	-	8.0-17.0	-
Greensand (Glauconite)	-	1.4	4.0-9.5
Rock phosphate (apatite)	-	38.0-40.0	-
Vegetative & Animal Concentrates			
Bonemeal, steamed	2.0	22.0	-
Castor pomace	6.0	1.9	0.5
Cocoa shell meal	2.5	1.5	2.5
Coffee grounds (dried)	2.0	0.04	0.7
Compost	0.5	0.5	0.5
Cottonseed meal	7.0	2.0	2.0
Dried blood meal	12.0	1.5	0.8
Eggshells	1.2	0.4	0.15
Fish meal	8.0	7.0	-
Fish scrap	7.0	3.0	-
Hoof & horn meal	12.0	2.0	-
Pine needles	0.5	0.1	0.3
Soybean meal	6.0	1.5	1.5
Wood ashes	-	1.8	5.0

Commercial or organic fertilizers can be sprinkled around transplants after they have been in the garden for about a week. Commercial fertilizers must be mixed into the soi . Organic fertilizers will not burn plants, but should be mixed in for more even distribution.

ing a more or less complete fertilizer capable of fulfilling all your plants' needs.

It all boils down to this: adding natural fertilizers makes your soil healthy. If your soil is healthy, your plants are going to be healthy, too. It is just that simple. Diseases and insects are less likely to attack strong, healthy plants than weak, spindly ones. If you use commer-

cial fertilizers year after year without putting in any organic matter, you are making a serious mistake. You are sapping the soil and are leaving yourself open to all sorts of trouble. You are providing the immediate chemical nutrients but not doing anything for the texture and structure of your soil or providing a favorable environment for the important soil organisms.

CHAPTER 8

CULTIVATION
AND KEEPING OUT WEEDS

CULTIVATION IS IMPORTANT! Most gardening books don't stress this enough. Cultivating lets oxygen get to the tiny microorganisms at work in the soil. They, in turn, will decompose the organic matter in the ground, releasing nutrients which the plants can use. Soil, like people, must be allowed to breathe. Cultivating once a week or so also creates a dust mulch, which will hold moisture in the ground.

You should begin to cultivate the soil as soon as your seedlings appear. This is the time when they need it most.

As you cultivate, remember that you should hoe, till, or scratch just the surface of the soil because so many garden plants have shallow feeder roots. Pull any weeds that don't fall victim to your cultivating tool. If they are allowed to grow, they will steal moisture and plant food from your vegetables. A garden filled with weeds will yield just about half as much as a well-kept garden of the same size.

Killing weeds between rows is no problem.

You can do it with a rotary tiller or with a hoe. Weeds within the row have to be pulled. As you pull them, keep a sharp eye out for diseased and dying vegetable plants. Pull these up too and dispose of them. If there seem to be a lot, try to find out what disease they have. Gardening books can be helpful, and so can the Agricultural Extension Service. They can tell you if you have a serious problem and can suggest what you should be doing about it. Don't panic if a few plants die. This may be normal attrition. There is probably little danger that a major outbreak of disease will destroy your whole crop.

A lot of people have asked me, "How do you tell the plants from the weeds?" This is not as silly as it might sound. It can be a big problem for inexperienced gardeners. Weed and vegetable seedlings may come up at exactly the same time. One thing you can do is keep the packet the seeds came in. This will give you a good picture of what the vegetable looks like when it is mature. From this, you can get

Keeping weeds out of your garden means your plants will not be robbed of moisture and nutrients. A hoe with one small finger will allow you to work near your plants without damaging them.

Be careful not to cut your plants off along with the weeds. If the back of your hoe stays pointed toward the plant you reduce the chances of a slip that will cause damage.

some idea of what it looks like when it is very young.

It's also a good idea to mark both ends of your rows with small wooden or plastic stakes. These should remind you where you have planted what. The greenery coming up elsewhere is probably weeds. If you plant in single rows, check to see which seedlings are coming up in a line. Weeds, naturally, don't grow in a straight row. In a wide row, the largest number of seedlings of the same type are probably your plants.

One of the best times to weed and cultivate is a few hours after a rain shower. Wait until the plants have dried off, then go into the garden before the ground gets too dry. Weeds pull up very easily because the ground is soft, and you will not risk disturbing the roots of neighboring vegetable plants. This is also an excellent time to cultivate. Weed seeds near the soil surface may have started to germinate as a result of the rainfall. If you expose them to the dry air and sun, they will die.

The In-Row Weeder

I have invented a tool that I call an in-row weeder. It is very handy, especially in wide-row plantings. You can rake right over the tops of plants with it. (You can also use a regular broom rake with round, spring teeth, but it won't work quite so well.) You can use the in-row weeder whenever the plants get to be half an inch to an inch tall. I start going over the plants once or twice a week at that time.

You can understand how the in-row weeding tool works if you understand a little about the way plants grow. When a seed begins to germinate, it sends down a deep root called the "tap root." Then the plant itself starts to

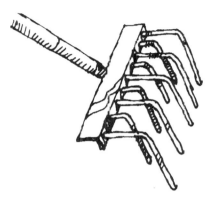

The in-row weeder developed by the author.

MULCHING TOMATOES

"I've found a good mulch for tomatoes. I collect large sheets of cardboard, and, after cutting holes and slits to put the plants through, I cover the ground around the plants with it. I never stake. This cardboard mulch keeps down weeds, holds moisture, keeps the fruit clean, and you can pick tomatoes without getting your feet dirty. In the fall, the cardboard will till into the soil."
SWR

grow upward. By the time it reaches the soil surface, tiny weeds have had time to grow, too. Unfortunately, these are too small to pull. What is fortunate is that the roots of these weeds grow very near the surface of the ground. Raking over a wide or single row with the weeder will pull up or disturb the roots of these little weeds before they have a chance to establish themselves. You will find that you will not pull up the vegetable plants because they are anchored by deep roots—unless they are planted too thickly, in which case the tool does a fine job of thinning. You will find that this little device can cut your weeding time in half.

Mulch Away the Weeds

A mulch is a layer of material spread on the garden so that it shades the ground. It prevents weeds from growing by depriving them of sunlight. It holds moisture in the soil by reducing evaporation, and it keeps the soil cooler on hot days and warmer on cool nights by acting as insulation.

You can use any number of things for mulch. You could try paper, sawdust, wood chips, grass clippings, hay, or polyethylene plastic. Mulching is particularly good in a small garden, where it will cut down on labor. It is a

A black, porous plastic mulch controls weeds. The mulch is laid down first and then holes are cut for planting. Usually mulches should be put on after planting when the ground has had a chance to warm up. But black plastic acts like a solar collector, so it can go on early. It is not very attractive, though, and natural materials, if available, also make good mulches.

Asparagus beds are one of the hardest parts of the vegetable garden to keep free of weeds. If you mulch with 6 inches of straw, the asparagus spears will come right up through in the spring. Peel back the mulch to cut them at ground level.

little harder in a very large garden simply because it is difficult to get enough mulch materials.

Grass clippings are one of the best and most common mulches. They contain no weed seeds. Let them dry for a day or two by spreading them in the sun. If you don't, they will get slimy and foul-smelling. Be careful about using old hay and straw as mulch. Try to get hay which was harvested before it had time to go to seed.

Remember that if mulch has weed seeds in it, it will surely add weeds to your garden. It will also attract rodents eager to feed on the seeds. Seedless organic mulches include grass clippings, leaves, wood chips, and salt marsh hay.

It is particularly important to use a seedless mulch around fruit trees and berry plants. Seeds will encourage rodents to crawl into the warm mulch for the winter. Once they have devoured the seeds, they will start to eat the berry canes or the bark from the trunks of the fruit trees.

Rodents sometimes damage vegetable crops, too. I like to grow at least some of my potatoes under a hay mulch. One year, when I used a seedy hay, I found that I had also raised several families of field mice in my potato patch. Those little fellows ate all the seeds in the hay, then chewed up almost all my potatoes.

If you mulch too early in the spring, you may find that it sets your crops back a week or two. Wait until the soil has warmed up in the late spring, then put mulch right around the stems of your plants, covering the ground completely. This should eliminate all weeding and cultivating.

The very best time to mulch is right after a heavy rain. If the mulch is thick enough, it will help the soil retain most of this moisture for the entire growing season.

A Full-Time Mulch

To build a permanent-mulch garden, stake off the boundaries of your plot, and till the soil until it is very loose and fine. Plant or transplant your vegetables as usual the first year. As soon as they come up and look healthy, spread mulch everywhere—in the rows, between the rows, and right up to the stems of the plants themselves. Protect the whole garden with it. As time goes on and the organic matter starts to decompose, add more mulch.

What you are doing is making it very difficult for weeds to grow. Those few that manage to poke through this heavy layer of organic matter will be easy to pull. When you do pull them up, drop them right in place so that they can become part of the mulch. A good mulch also provides a barrier which slows down evaporation. Permanent-mulch gardens almost never have to be watered.

Don't bother to till the soil at all the second year. You can lay out your rows and rake the mulch back just enough to make plantings. Once the plants have sprouted and grown a couple of inches tall, pull the mulch back around them. You will find that the soil beneath the mulch has stayed loose and friable because you have created an environment which is both appetizing to earthworms and hospitable to beneficial microorganisms of all kinds. If the mulch is heavy enough to keep the garden from freezing, they will work happily in your soil all year long.

To have a permanent-mulch garden, you have to have enough mulch! I mean enough to spread as much as 8 to 10 inches of it everywhere. It will settle to a depth of 4 to 7 inches. Use hay, straw, grass clippings, or leaves. I don't recommend using sawdust. If you do, you will have to add fertilizer to replace the nitrogen that the sawdust will use up as it decomposes. Most gardens with a permanent mulch don't require a lot of fertilizer, but there is no harm in adding a little when you pull the mulch back from the rows in spring.

It is hard to maintain a permanent mulch in a very large garden because it takes mountains of material to keep the area covered. A permanent mulch might also shorten your growing season a little. Mulched soil will stay cold and wet in the spring because the warming rays of the sun never strike it directly. This will delay the planting of heat-loving plants like tomatoes.

Year-round mulching has its advantages and disadvantages. In a small garden where you don't have to constantly scramble around to find enough mulch, it will certainly save you lots of work. The idea of permanent mulching was made famous by two books, *How to Have a Green Thumb Without an Aching Back* and

Straw has been used around these onions for mulch. Onions are very shallow-rooted and can dry out quickly. This mulch is only about 1 inch thick and was put in place the same day the onion sets were planted so that they would grow up through it.

HARVESTING SPUDS AND ROSEBUDS

"One year, my wife had about 400 roses which we mulched with shavings and hay. One spring, I bought 45 cents worth of seed potatoes and hid them in the rose mulch. At first, my wife was displeased with this, but when she discovered what lovely, clean potatoes were there, without digging, her mind was changed. She soon began moving the mulch, picking up the spuds, and hiding the smaller ones away in the mulch. We had plenty of potatoes the next year with no plowing or hoeing, and a new crop was harvested that way every year thereafter. I think that was about the best 45 cents I every spent." JG

Gardening Without Work, both written by Ruth Stout.

It is a good idea to mulch some portions of a large garden. Whenever plants get to be 5 or 6 inches high, you can bring mulch up around their stems. This will save you a lot of weeding,

Organic Mulches at a Glance

Mulch Material	Appearance	Insulation Value	Relative Cost	Thickness	Weed Control
Buckwheat hulls	Good	Good	High	1–1½ inches	Good — may sprout
Compost	Fair	Good	High — limited supply in most places	1–3 inches	Good
Grass clippings	Poor if not dried; can have unpleasant odor	Good	Low	1 inch maximum	Fair
Green ground covers (cover crops)	Fair	Good – once there is a heavy sod	Low	Allow to grow to full height	Good
Hay	Poor – unless chopped	Good	Low — especially if spoiled	6–8 inches; 2–3 inches if chopped	Good
Leaves	Fair	Good	Low	4–6 inches	Good
Leaf mold	Fair	Good	Low	1½ inches	Fair to good
Paper	Poor — can be covered with soil	Fair	Low — though high if purchased in rolls specifically for mulching	One to several thicknesses	Good
Peat moss	Good	Good	Moderate to high	1 inch	Good
Salt hay	Good	Good	Moderate — unless you gather it yourself	3–6 inches	Good — contains no seed
Seaweed, Kelp	Poor	Good — recommended as winter mulch	Low in coastal areas	4–6 inches	Excellent
Straw	Fair — unless chopped	Good	Low to moderate	6–8 inches; 1–2 inches if chopped	Good — but avoid oat straw for weed control

Organic Mulches (continued)

Mulch Material	Water Penetration	Water Retention in Soil	Speed of Decomposition	Other Remarks
Buckwheat hulls	Excellent	Fair	Slow	Easy to handle. Can be blown around in high winds or splashed by rain.
Compost	Good if well decomposed	Good	Rapid — adds many nutrients	Partially decomposed compost is an excellent feeding mulch.
Grass clippings	Good if not matted	Fair	Rapid — green grass adds nitrogen	Can be mixed with peat moss. After drying can be spread thinly around young plants.
Green ground covers (cover crops)	Good	Good	Decomposing legumes and cover crops are nitrogen-rich	Should be harvested or tilled directly into the soil.
Hay	Good	Good	Rapid — adds nitrogen	Can be mixed with peat moss. After drying can be spread thinly around young plants.
Leaves	Fair — likely to mat	Good	Fairly slow — contributes nitrogen	Adds many valuable nutrients. Can be chopped and mixed with other things.
Leaf mold	Fair — if too thick will prevent percolation	Good	Rapid	An excellent feeding mulch.
Paper	Poor — unless perforated	Good	Slow — unless designed to be biodegradable	Can be shredded and used effectively.
Peat moss	Poor — can absorb many times its weight in water	Poor — may draw moisture from the soil	Very slow	Adds little or no nutrients to the soil. Valuable only as a soil conditioner.
Salt hay	Good — does not mat	Good	Slow	Can be used year after year. Is pest-free. Good for winter protection.
Seaweed, Kelp	Fair	Good	Slow — adds nitrogen and potash	Provides sodium, boron, and other trace elements. Excellent for sheet composting.
Straw	Good	Good	Fairly slow — nitrogen fertilizer is helpful	Should be seed-free if possible. Straw is highly flammable.

Make a slight depression in the mulch mound surrounding your plants to catch rainwater.

For a good crop of potatoes, the plants must be constantly buried so that just the top few leaves remain above the surface. This also buries weeds. Tomatoes, corn, and beans also benefit from some hilling, although you shouldn't bury them like potatoes.

hoeing, and cultivating in the rows. If you do not have enough material to mulch between the rows, limit yourself to mulching around the plants. Most organic mulches add nutrients to the soil, so when you mulch you are also side-dressing. Earthworms and microorganisms will eventually devour organic mulches and turn them into good humus. When the gardening season is over, you can simply turn under all remaining mulch along with crop residues if you don't want to maintain a permanent mulch.

Some crops are a lot easier to take care of when they are mulched. Mulching the area where your cucumber or squash vines are going to grow, for instance, will save you the headache of having to weed later on, when the plants are spread out over the ground. Once the soil has warmed up, you will probably want to mulch at least some of your tomato and pepper plants. The mulch will keep the earth around these plants' roots at a more even temperature, which they like. You might also want to mulch your sweet corn. Some plants are not worth mulching. Carrots and beets are difficult because you can only put mulch on either side of the row. You can, of course, mulch the plants with some sort of finely chopped material, but I think it is more work than it is worth. There is no reason to mulch most peas; they ripen early in the spring and are usually finished by the time the heavy weed season comes along. Pea vines themselves, however, make a nourishing mulch for other plants, especially if they are shredded or chopped. You might want to use them around your tomatoes. The timing is just about perfect. The peas will be spent by the time the tomatoes are ready for mulch.

The very best mulches are alfalfa, clover, and all the other legumes, including peas and beans. All legumes have a high nitrogen content and contribute nitrogen to the soil both when they are growing and after they are dead. This is why they are the most nearly perfect mulch you can use. The plants are almost as precious as the food they produce. I think trying to find some alfalfa or clover hay would be worth your while, even if you have to pay a little for it.

Some people call mulching a "sophisticated" gardening technique. I disagree. It can be as simple or as complicated as you want to make it. Almost every good gardener mulches some things. Some do a lot more than others. You should do as much as seems practical to you.

Grass clippings, as well as cut alfalfa hay and clover, make excellent mulches if they are allowed to dry out before using them on the garden. They add nitrogen to the soil as they decompose. If you are using herbicides on your lawn, avoid using grass clippings in the garden for at least a week to allow the herbicides to break down.

CHAPTER 9

TAKING CARE
OF YOUR PLANTS

An old-fashioned watering can is a good investment. It puts the water where you want it in a gentle shower and comes in handy at transplanting time.

WOULD YOU BELIEVE ME IF I told you that I never water my garden? It's true. The only time I water is when I transplant. I give new plants water for a couple of days after they have been set out, then I leave them alone. I guess I am fortunate to have excellent soil which is rich in humus and holds moisture well.

I will grant that most gardens need to be watered at one time or another, but I am discouraged to see so many gardeners watering unwisely. Too many people look out the window, see some of their plants wilting on a hot afternoon, and rush out to water them. A lot of plants will droop in a strong, hot sun late in the day. This is normal. It is a different story if the plants still look wilted when you get up in the morning. When plants look drought-stricken early in the day, you should give them some water.

But don't water just for the sake of watering. Water only when it is really necessary. You are doing more harm than good when you

AVERAGE SUMMER PRECIPITATION
(June-August)

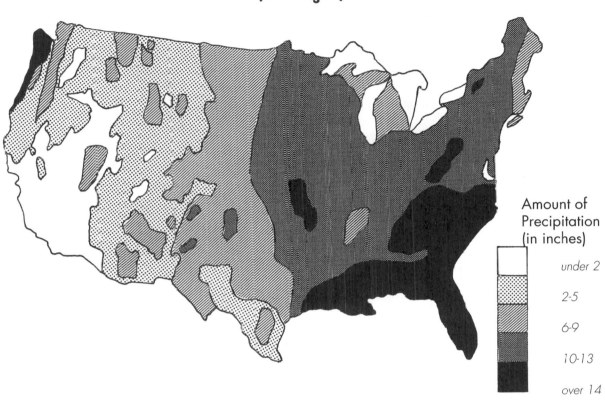

Amount of
Precipitation
(in inches)

under 2

2-5

6-9

10-13

over 14

sprinkle water on the garden just to keep the dust down or to moisten the soil surface. You should encourage your plants' roots to grow as deep as possible. If the plants get used to finding water near the soil surface, they will grow only shallow roots. When it really gets dry, these plants will not survive. If you are going to water, don't pussyfoot around. Soak the soil. Make sure that it is very wet at least 3 to 6 inches below the surface.

Watering

Ideally, a garden should get 1 inch of rain or applied water per week. Applying 1 inch of water to an acre takes 27,000 gallons. You can use this figure to determine the cost of apply-

ing an inch of water to your garden if you know its approximate size.

One good way to water is with a "soaker," a perforated canvas hose which allows water to run directly into the ground. An overhead sprinkler works well if you leave it in one place long enough, but I don't use these if I can help it, especially on a hot day. Sprinklers seem to use up a lot more water because so much moisture evaporates before it reaches the ground.

Watering Corn

Corn can use plenty of water, but this isn't true of all crops. Cantaloupes don't like an abundance of water. They crack, and their flavor is

On tomato plants, "suckers" will form between the main stem and the leaf branches. These should be removed by pinching them off. If they are big, carefully cut them.

not good if they are given too much water. Tomatoes shouldn't be overwatered, either.

Cultivate Before Irrigating

Before irrigating or watering your garden, cultivate wherever the soil has been packed hard by walking or by equipment. If you don't, water will cause a hard solid crust to form and seal out both air and water. Of course, this is not as important on very sandy soils. Remember that a lot of organic matter in the soil will keep it from packing.

Furrow or Row Irrigation

Row irrigation, which is done by running water in furrows between rows of plants, is an excellent method of watering where conditions permit. The only equipment necessary is a hose or pipe and a wooden trough for distributing water to several furrows at once.

Row irrigation works best on land with a slope of 2 to 6 inches of fall per 100 feet, but it can be adapted to land with more or with less slope. On very steep slopes, small furrow streams must be used to prevent erosion. If the soil surface is uneven or extremely flat, you may have to grade the garden (move soil from one area to another) to make row irrigation possible. The size of the wooden trough will vary according to the number of rows you want to irrigate at once and the capacity of your hose or pipe. Usually, a flow of 1 to 5 gallons per minute for each hole will be necessary. Drill holes 1 inch in diameter on one side of the trough near the bottom. The holes should be the same distance apart as the furrows. It is also a good idea to attach a wooden knob just above each hole so the flow of water can be easily adjusted or stopped. In order to get an even distribution of water in the furrow, adjust the flow so that water reaches the end of the furrow in about one-fourth of the time it takes to irrigate the whole row. Water is therefore on the lower end of the row three-fourths as long as it is on the upper end.

Start irrigating with a heavy flow of water; then turn back the water so that an even flow is maintained in the row with no puddling or washing at the end of the row. Check the depth to which the water has penetrated with a shovel, a steel rod or a stick. Water that seeps down deeper than the root zone is wasted.

Pruning

Tomatoes

Pruning and training tomato plants properly keeps them producing longer and favorably affects the size and quality of the fruit. There are many different methods of training, but the most common is staking. As the plant grows, it is tied with strips of cloth, old nylon stockings, or soft cord to a 6-foot-tall wooden stake. Early in the growing season, probably in June, pruning should begin. In the angle where each leaflet branch joins the main stem, a sucker or side shoot will grow. All of these should be pinched out as soon as they appear. At first, you may have to prune once a week; later, once every two weeks may be adequate. Once the plant reaches the top of the stake, you can pinch out the growing tip to stop further vertical growth. Or you can discontinue pruning, and allow all new suckers to grow without staking. They will fall over, set some fruit, and provide shade for the fruit on the rest of the plant.

The "Missouri Method" of pruning is very similar to the one described above. Its advocates claim that this method produces yield increases of 15 to 25 percent (as a result of larger fruits). Stake, tie, and remove suckers as above, but do not remove any sucker that is growing directly below a flower cluster. As soon as each of these remaining suckers gets

Choose a soft material for tying up tomato plants. Strips of cloth, old nylon stockings, or soft twine can be used. Make a loop around the plant below a branch, and tie the material firmly to the stake or it will slide down. As the tomato plant grows, continue the process by placing a new tie every 6 to 8 inches up the stake.

GARDEN PROBLEM GUIDE

Symptoms	Possible Causes	Possible Cures
Dying young plants	Fertilizer burn	Mix fertilizer thoroughly with soil.
	Disease (damping-off)	Treat seed; don't overwater.
Stunted plants (pale to yellow)	Low soil fertility	Soil test for fertilizer recommendations.
	Low soil pH (too acid)	Soil test for lime recommendations.
	Poor soil drainage	Drain and add organic matter.
	Shallow or compacted soil	Plow deeper.
	Insects or diseases	Identify and use control measures.
	Nematodes	Soil test for treatment recommendations.
Stunted plants (purplish color)	Low temperature	Plant at recommended time.
	Lack of phosphorus	Add phosphorus fertilizer.
Holes in leaves	Insects	Identify and use control measures.
	Hail	Be thankful it was not worse.
Spots, molds, or darkened areas on leaves and stems	Disease	Identify, spray or dust, use resistant varieties.
	Chemical burn	Use recommended chemical at recommended rate.
	Fertilizer burn	Keep fertilizer off plants.
Wilting plants	Dry soil	Irrigate if possible.
	Excess water in soil	Drain.
	Nematodes	Soil test for treatment recommendations.
	Disease	Use resistant varieties if possible.
Weak, spindly plants	Too much shade	Remove shade or move plants to sunny spot.
	Too much water	Drain or avoid overwatering.
	Plants too thick	Seed at recommended rate.
	Too much nitrogen	Avoid excess fertilization.
Failure to set fruit	High temperature	Follow recommended planting time.
	Low temperature	Follow recommended planting time.
	Too much nitrogen	Avoid excess fertilization.
	Insects	Identify and use control measures.
Tomato leaf curl	Heavy pruning in hot weather	Don't.
	Disease	Identify and use control measures.
Dry brown to black rot on blossom end of tomato	Low soil calcium	Add lime.
	Extremely dry soil	Irrigate.
Misshapen tomatoes ("catfacing")	Cool weather during blooming	Plant at recommended time.
Abnormal leaves and growth	2,4-D weed killer	Don't use a sprayer that has previously applied 2,4-D.
	Virus disease	Remove infected plants to prevent spreading. Control insects that transmit viruses.

about 6 inches long, you should then pinch off the growing tip. These extra branches increase the plant's food-producing capacity and provide some shading for the tender fruits.

Still another variation is the double-stem system, in which all suckers except the first one directly below the first flower cluster are removed. This first sucker is allowed to develop into a second stem. Both stems are tied to the same stake, and all other suckers are removed as soon as they appear. Tomato plants grown in wire cylinders or similar support structures don't need to be pruned. Neither do unsupported tomatoes.

Some tomato varieties have what is called a *determinate* growth habit, which means they form short, bushy plants usually less than 3 feet tall. These plants require little or no pruning. Some determinate varieties are: Springset, Roma, Small Fry, Fireball, New Yorker, and Spring Giant.

Melons, Squash, and Pumpkins

These vegetables also benefit from pruning. Pruning consists simply of picking the fuzzy green growing tips off the vines. This keeps the plants from taking up too much garden space and forces them to devote more of their growing energy to fruit production. If the climate in your part of the country is so cold that

Here is a Brussels sprout "palm tree" made by breaking off lower leaves as the sprouts form. This directs the plant's energy into forming sprouts, not foliage. As the end of the season approaches, cut off the very top of the plant to stop upward growth and direct even more energy into forming more and bigger sprouts.

To get melons to ripen faster, I place the small ones on old coffee cans. This gets them up off the cool ground and out of the shade of the foliage where they can warm up. The can helps keep them warm.

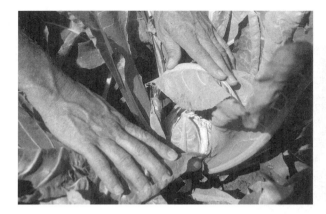

If heads of cauliflower are exposed to the sun they will turn dark, purple, and bitter. Watch for small heads to appear. When they are the size of a tennis ball, break the main stem of the largest surrounding leaves and fold them over the heads to keep them shaded. Keep an eye on them and you'll harvest tasty, white heads four or five days later. You can also gather the leaves around the head and tie them or secure them with a rubber band.

GROWING CARROTS IN RICE HULLS

"One spring we purchased several bales of rice hulls to put around our strawberries. During this time we were planting our garden.

"Since our ground gets hard and is very difficult to grow root crops in, we thought we would try something different. We planted carrots, beets, and radishes in the following manner: After tilling the ground, we used our furrowing attachment to dig a furrow approximately 6 to 7 inches deep. We filled this to about 3 inches from the top with rice hulls. Then we spread a very thin layer of dirt to lay the seed on. I planted the seed and covered with another layer of dirt. And then the harvest! We had the best crop of beets and carrots we ever raised!

"The rice hulls hold moisture and keep the ground loose so the root crops can grow bigger." PS

If you have water running down a weedy field or pasture, and then across your garden, you'll have lots of weeds, regardless of how clean you keep your garden. Weed seeds will be carried by the water.

frost frequently destroys a large part of your melon harvest, you can speed up the ripening process by pruning judiciously. Around the first week in August (when the melons are probably just starting to ripen), pick the fuzzy ends off all the vines. Then, during the last week in August, pick off any melons that are too small and green to ripen before frost. All the plant's energy can now go to the fruit still on the vine. (Keep picking off the fuzzy vine ends.)

If you water your garden with a sprinkler, you should know how long it must run to deliver an inch of water. To find out, set a few cans at various distances from the sprinkler and turn it on. Measure the water in the cans periodically, and take note of how long it takes for an inch of water to accumulate in the various cans. (It will probably take longer than you think.)

CHAPTER 10

A GALLERY
OF GARDENING TECHNIQUES

I. TESTING SEED GERMINATION

Are those leftover seeds any good? Many seeds are viable for up to five years if they are stored at temperatures around 40° to 50°F. (4° to 10°C.) in a relatively dry location. If you plan to store seeds, seal the individual seed packets after planting all the seeds you need in the garden, then place the packets in a plastic bag and seal it. Store these bags in a covered coffee can in the basement or some other cool, dry place.

1. Dampen a double thickness of paper towel and place ten seeds of each type you are testing on it. Identify which varieties you are testing by including pieces of the seed packet or slips of paper with the seed variety names written on them.

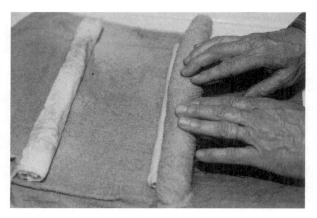

2. Roll up the paper towel. Make as many paper towel rolls as necessary. Then roll the paper up in a damp cloth towel. You can get several paper rolls in each towel, but they should not touch each other.

3. Seal the towel in a plastic bag with holes punched in it for ventilation. Put it in a warm place where you won't forget about it. The top of the refrigerator is a good choice.

II. GARDENING IN SMALL SPACES

1-2. Growing up instead of out is one way to get the most out of a small vegetable garden like this one. Instead of sprawling, cucumbers are trained up chicken wire supported by a frame of 1" x 3" lumber. The wire is sandwiched between two pieces of lumber. The frame is held at an angle by legs from the frame to the ground. The legs are nailed to stakes driven into the ground.

4. Check your seeds in five to seven days. Germinating seeds will have bulged and sent out a shoot. If the germination rate is less than 50 percent, you'll have to sow twice as heavily in the row to make up for it. Don't continue to store seeds with low germination rates.

3-5. Pole beans will climb up coarse twine. Here, 8-foot poles are set into the ground with at least 6 feet of pole above the ground. Twine or wire runs along the tops of the poles and a parallel piece runs along the bottoms about 4 inches above the ground. Vertical pieces stretch from top to bottom about a foot apart. You might be able to use this idea around a patio as a shade or privacy screen. You can also grow pole beans up a tepee of four poles. Plant four or five bean seeds in a circle at the base of each pole. A summer crop of lettuce can be grown in the shade under the tepee.

6. A mixture of flowers and vegetables can be grown in containers, as in this flower box near my patio. The containers must have a place for water to drain out of the bottom. Place stones, broken flower pots, crushed rock, or similar materials at the bottom to help with drainage. Then use a few inches of garden soil topped with a layer of soilless mix. Keep an eye on the plants during hot weather; they may have to be watered every day.

7-8. Onions, tomatoes, herbs, cukes . . . 13 different vegetables growing in half a whiskey barrel. Or plant a barrel for a kitchen-door herb or salad garden. Or plant all tomatoes. Just remember to provide for drainage and make sure to keep the plants well watered, especially during hot weather. Barrels are available at many garden centers. Look for plant varieties specifically created for small-space growing, such as Pixie and Patio tomatoes and bush cucumbers.

III. BUILDING RAISED BEDS

Raised beds are often used in heavy soil like clay to get roots up and away from standing water, but they can be used in other soils, too. Raised beds warm up faster in the spring and can give you a head start on the growing season. If you have a small garden, you can make your raised beds permanent. They don't even have to be straight. They can be curved to take advantage of the sun or the contour of the land.

1. Start by thoroughly tilling or turning over the soil to make it as easy to work as possible. I make my rows 2 feet wide and mark them with stakes and cord. First I walk down one side and pull soil up from the far side.

2. Then I reverse sides and pull soil up from where I had been standing. Pull plenty of soil up over the top of the cord. Taking 2 inches out of each walkway will give you a 4-inch-high bed.

3. Level off the top of the row.

4. Repeat the process right down the garden. The raised bed can be 4 to 8 inches high.

5. Plant raised beds the same way you would plant a wide row. Broadcast seeds along the top and tap them in with the back of your hoe. Bring soil up from the walkways with a rake to bury the seeds, even off the bed, and tap again with the back of the hoe to make sure the seeds are in firm contact with the soil.

IV. PLANT WIDE ROWS FOR PRODUCTIVITY

You want to get the most harvest out of the least amount of space, right? So do I, even though I have lots of room. That's why I plant nearly everything in wide rows, super-wide rows, multi-plantings, and blocks. A wide row will give you two to three times the harvest of the old single-file row. Just as importantly, as these wide rows and blocks grow, they form a living mulch that shades out the weeds and shades in the moisture. Here's what they look like.

1. A comparison of a single row and a wide row of beans. I plant my wide rows a garden rake's width—about 16 inches—across. This makes it handy for marking and planting, but wide rows can be made wider. Twenty inches is another good width.

3. When your cabbage, cauliflower, or head lettuce fills in it will look like this . . . a solid block of productivity. It is work-free, because the heads form a living mulch to keep weeds down and hold in moisture.

2. Cabbages, cauliflower, and head lettuce can be planted in a row 20 inches wide in a staggered pattern like this. Plant three across, move down the row 8 inches and in 5 inches from each side of the row, and plant two across. This should space the plants 10 inches apart. Then move down and plant three, and so on.

4. A wide row of lettuce 3 feet long will be plenty for a family of four. To harvest, cut the plants with a knife just above the ground. It will grow back to give you a second and third harvest. Compare the wide row to the single row next to it and you'll get an idea of the increased harvest.

5. I plant up to a hundred onion sets in 1 foot of a row 3 feet wide. Begin to use them as scallions. That allows the onions remaining in the ground to expand. Big Bermuda onions need a little more room—3 to 4 inches between each set. One pound of onion sets contains 130 to 150 onions.

6. Peas and beans can be planted in "plant-and-pick" blocks 6 or even 10 feet across. The secret is in the harvesting. Take a three-legged stool with you and work your way through the patch. Blocks are good for harvest gardens, where you plan to freeze enough for the winter.

7. This is a multi-row that contains radishes, onions, spinach, and two kinds of lettuce. You could grow an entire salad garden in one wide row if you added a few tomato plants at the ends of the row.

V. SUCCESSION PLANTING

1. There's no need to have a bare spot in your garden after you harvest early crops like the lettuce and onions I'm taking here from a multi-row. Letting the sun hit bare soil during the growing season is a waste of solar energy. Plant a succession crop for a late summer or fall harvest.

2. Simply turn the soil over, turning in any remaining plant material. You could add a little organic fertilizer to the row. I'm going to plant beets, so adding a cup of bonemeal would be good, since root crops like phosphorus. Simply sprinkle it evenly over the row.

   After leveling off the soil, I'll pull my garden rake straight down the row. It will leave a mark that will become the row.

3-4. Sprinkle the seeds in the row and then pat down the soil by hand. I bury the seeds with about four times their diameter of soil, then pat it down again. Water the seeds and watch how fast they come up during the warm summer months.

VI. STRETCHING THE SEASON, SPRING AND FALL

1. It's already summer inside my sun pit greenhouse, although the grass outside is just turning green. These plants, started from seed in February and March, will be set out into the garden after the last frost, which comes in April or May here in Vermont. Starting my own plants saves time and money because of the large number of vegetables I grow. But it also helps you stretch the season and grow varieties that you may not be able to find for sale later on at the garden center or nursery.

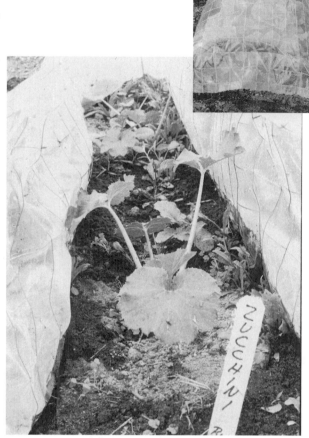

2. Tomatoes like warm conditions. These pleated plastic sleeves are filled with water, which heats up during the day and keeps the plants warm on cool spring nights.

3-4. Plants like zucchini, melons, and cucumbers can be started in rows directly in the garden up to two weeks before the last frost. Create a mini-greenhouse of plastic sheeting reinforced with wire. Bury the edges to hold them down. Even on cool days, the sun will quickly warm up the plants inside of these tunnels.

5. Tender plants like tomatoes need to be protected if you gamble by setting them out before or close to the last frost date. You may have to use hotcaps like these to cover them when a frost threatens. These are from a garden center, but you can make your own by cutting the bottoms out of plastic milk jugs.

6. In the North, you can grow sweet potatoes by first cutting the potatoes in half and then placing them in a pan of moist soilless mix. Then set them in a warm place out of direct light. Very slowly, sprouts will develop. After the soil outside warms up, plant these sprouts in the garden 4 or 5 inches deep.

7-8. You can grow fresh onions on your windowsill anytime. Fill a container three-quarters full with soilless mix. Then pack in onion sets so they are touching and cover them with mix. Gently firm them down and water them. Place in a sunny spot. Pull them for use as scallions whenever you need them, and the remaining onions will have room to expand. You can get up to 65 sets into a single 8-inch pot.

9-10. Turnips, scallions, carrots, parsnips, cabbage, beets, kale, Brussels sprouts, and leeks can all be harvested from underneath the snow early in the winter. Snow actually protects plants from killing subzero temperatures. Carrots and parsnips can be stored right in the ground by covering them with a 12- to 18-inch-thick mulch of straw or leaves. Harvest them as you need them. Be sure to recover the remaining vegetables with mulch after each harvest.

CHAPTER 11

GARDENING
WITH NATURE

HAVING YOUR OWN GARDEN gives you the control over what is in the food you eat. The small-scale gardener does not have to rely on a regular application of pesticides to produce the picture-perfect vegetables we see in the supermarket.

It seems that just about every week we are presented with another frightening story about pesticides. Mothers concerned about cancer in children have organized to fight pesticides. Vegetables imported into the U.S. are treated with pesticides that are banned in this country. Our food is being trucked in containers that carry chemicals one way and food the other.

If you are going to garden, there will be times when you are bugged by insects. But as a home gardener you can develop a bug-beating battle plan that steers clear of pesticides.

Basics about Bugs

Not every bug is a bad bug. Yes, some are in your garden to chew on your vegetables. But many others are there to eat the bugs that eat your vegetables. You may have to get over some age-old prejudices about things that crawl, but among the gardener's best friends are earthworms, spiders, and toads.

The insects that harm your vegetables come in three basic varieties:

1. Insects that eat leaves or suck plant juices from stems.
2. Insects that feed from within the stems themselves.
3. Insects that attack at ground level or below the surface of the soil.

The best time to stop bugs is before they have had a chance to multiply. Catch them as the insect larvae are starting to hatch.

Work with Nature to Battle Bugs

It's easy to develop a strategy for dealing with bugs if you are aware of some of the choices available. You can start with the least severe action and get tougher only as necessary. The following sections offer some useful weapons in the battle against bugs.

Healthy Soil and Healthy Plants

Bugs will go after weak and unhealthy plants. As I mentioned earlier, success starts from the ground up. Healthy soil and healthy plants mean less damage from bugs, and a healthy plant will usually survive a bug attack. Choose disease-resistant seeds and you will reduce bug problems at the same time.

Think Again about Bug Damage

Some bug damage to plants and even crops is acceptable. You don't want to encourage an invasion of your garden, but don't panic if you see some plants with holes chewed in the leaves. Follow some of the steps below. And, if you're concerned about a vegetable with a small amount of bug damage, keep in mind how much pesticide it takes to produce acres of a crop untouched by bugs. By comparison, a little bug damage is better for you

Good Garden Housekeeping

Rotate crops and get rid of places where bugs might breed or winter over. Slug problems can be reduced if you keep the grass short around your garden, because they hide in tall grass during the day. Clean out and turn over your garden in the fall to remove breeding grounds. Dispose of bug-infested garden material some distance away from your garden. You may also be able to plan your planting to avoid insect cycles. Early crops have more problems than fall crops.

Pick Them Off

The most direct attack is to pick the bugs off or knock them off into a container of water with a little soap, oil, or kerosene in it. If you see damage but no bug, turn the leaf over and check the back. Some insects do their damage at night, so a trip to the garden with a flashlight often leads to the culprit. Also, check the backs of leaves for eggs, and crush them. For slugs, put a few boards out in the garden. During the day, when the slugs are hiding, turn the board over and squash them or sprinkle a little salt on them. With the vine crops, you may find that insects congregate on one plant over the course of two or three days. Remove the plant and the bugs if you find one that is a bug target. Burn them if you can, but be sure to crush the bugs if you can't.

Traps

Insects like slugs and earwigs hide in dark, damp places during the day. An old garden hose, cut into foot-long sections and strung together on lengths of cord, can be used as a trap. Clean the sections into a bucket of soapy water every few days. After you've had your grapefruit or cantaloupe for breakfast, turn the half rinds upside down in the garden for traps. Place saucers of beer in the garden to trap slugs. Try loosely covering them to reduce evaporation and dilution by rain. Japanese beetle traps are available in garden centers. Place them some distance away from your garden so you don't attract every beetle in the area to your garden.

Beneficial Insects

Ladybugs prey on aphids, eggs of Colorado potato beetles, and spider mites. The praying mantis will eat aphids, beetles, leafhoppers, caterpillars, and wasps. Ladybug and mantis egg cases can be purchased by mail. Look for ads in magazines like *Organic Gardening* or *National Gardening*. The diamond-shaped assassin bugs prey on potato and bean beetles, and spiders eat anything they can. Some of the lesser-known beneficial insects are hover flies (which prey on aphids, mealybugs, and leafhoppers), ant lions (ants and small insects), and dragonflies and damselflies (mosquitoes). There is no way to guarantee that these beneficial insects will stay in your garden, however.

Birds

Except for crows, most birds in your garden have their eye out for bugs. Maybe that explains why many bugs work at night or hide on the bottoms of leaves. Years ago, every big garden had a purple martin house on a pole in the middle of the garden or at least nearby. When it comes to fruits and berries, however, birds can take a heavy toll. If you want to attract birds, try putting a birdbath in or near your garden. Keep the water in it fresh and clear.

Companion Planting

There is more myth than science in the area of companion planting. Some people swear by it, others don't think it works. I don't count on it, but my feeling is: if it works for you, do it. The idea is that some plants repel insects, so you should mix them in with your vegetables. Marigolds, asters, cosmos, and coreopis are reported to repel insects. If you're going to plant flowers in your garden for color, you might as well try these. Members of the aster family seem to repel insects.

Home Remedies

Many gardeners make their own sprays to repel insects. Some of the remedies I've heard of can be as toxic as pesticides, so stick to natural ingredients for your own spray recipe. Here's a repellent spray you can make in your blender:

1 medium-sized onion
1 teaspoon very hot red pepper
3 cloves garlic, peeled
1 quart water

Strain the blended mixture through cheese-cloth or an old nylon stocking and spray it on. It will also freeze well for later use.

Molasses works very well for sucking or chewing insects. Mix one part molasses with 50 parts water so you can spray it. It will stick to the bugs. Another spray can be made with laundry soap (**not** detergent). Mix ⅛ to ¼ pound with 2 gallons of water, and spray the plants. You can add hot pepper and vegetable oil (to stick) for good measure, if you wish. Onion, garlic, hot Chinese mustard, cloves, and ginger are other choices for spray ingredients. Be sure to spray under the leaves. Some people even collect bugs, grind them up with water, then strain and spray them back onto the plants to repel their insect compatriots.

Learn to Love a Toad

If toads were as cute as kittens, everyone would have a few around the house, because they are very useful. Before pesticides, housewives kept them indoors to catch cockroaches and other insects. They are bug-eating machines and one of the few predators that eats slugs. In three months, a single toad will eat up to 10,000 insects and cutworms. In parts of Europe, toads were brought to market and sold to horticulturists. One U.S. golf course used to charge one toad as admission to Saturday morning kids' movies. Toads feed at night and hide during the day. Toad houses can be made from cracked flowerpots turned upside down and sunk into the ground with an inch or so above ground. Break a hole at ground level for an entrance. Toads drink through their skin, so they must have a basin or puddle or pond near the garden. I found out how to attract toads by accident. One day a plastic water line sprung a leak, so I wrapped a large rag around it to stop it from spraying. Several days later I returned to fix it permanently and found a collection of toads clinging to the water-soaked rag like a bunch of grapes. The break was in a shady, overgrown place, not out in the open. Toads are territorial, so if you move them into your garden, provide shelter and water and pen them up for a few days. Toads are probably the most underrated bug control method available to home gardeners, but they can operate only at ground level and a few inches above

Natural Pesticides

Pesticides found in nature are a good choice when things get out of hand. One advantage of these is that very often they work on only one insect or one type of insect, therefore sparing ones you may want to encourage in your garden. They also break down faster than synthetics. These advantages turn out to be a disadvantage for a commercial grower or the gardener who does not want to take the time to distinguish between bugs. Some of the most popular broad-spectrum insecticides, like those containing carbaryl, kill just about everything, including honeybees. Here are some examples of insecticides found in nature or derived from natural sources:

Bt, or Bacillus thuringiensis. A microbial insecticide that kills caterpillars and caterpillar-like worms including cabbage loopers, tent caterpillars, and gypsy moths in their caterpillar stage. Bt is widely available. Often sold under the name Dipel, it has no toxic effect on bees, pets, or humans. It kills by paralyzing the insect's digestive track.

Milky spore disease powder. Japanese beetles emerge from grubs in your lawn. This bacterium attacks them in their grub stage, but Japanese beetles get around, and milky spore will not prevent them from arriving from your neighbor's yard. Traps may also be required if infestations are heavy.

Rotenone, ryania, and pyrethrum are insecticides derived from plants themselves.

Rotenone is an extract from the roots of derris and cubé. It is a stomach and contact poison that kills beetles, aphids, loopers, thrips, earworms, and many other bugs. Rotenone may also be found in pet stores or at veterinary clinics, since it kills some common external animal parasites. But it also kills bees and is very toxic to fish.

Pyrethrum is a contact insecticide from the flower heads of the pyrethrum chrysanthemum. It is effective against flying insects because it knocks down and stuns them. Use pyrethrum against leafhoppers, thrips, flies, aphids, and other flying insects.

Ryania is a resin extracted from ground ryania shrub stems. It is a stomach poison effective against many of the leaf-eating insects and the corn borer. It can be used on apple trees against the codling moth, with about a half dozen applications necessary per season.

Bt, rotenone, and pyrethrum and a mixture of rotenone and pyrethrum can be found at well-stocked garden centers. Ryania is harder to find. Bonide Chemical Company of Yorkville, New York, is a producer of both organic and synthetic pesticides found in many retail stores.

Just because a substance is "natural" or "organic" does not mean it lacks punch. The

VEGETABLE INSECTS

Insect	Crop	Spray Formula	Remarks
APHID	Cabbage Cucumbers Melons Peas Peppers Potatoes Tomatoes	Insecticidal soaps. Pyrethrum spray.	Apply on foliage when aphids appear. Repeat weekly as needed. Natural enemies include ladybugs and aphid lions, the larvae of the lacewing.
BLISTER BEETLE	Potatoes Corn Tomatoes Beans	Rotenone spray.	
CABBAGE WORM	Broccoli Cabbage Cauliflower Greens	*Bacillus thuringiensis* (Bt), a biological insecticide.	Thorough treatment is necessary. Repeat weekly as needed. Begin treatment when worms are small. Eggs are laid by white butterflies. Hard to see to hand-pick, but you will see chewed leaves and their dark droppings.
CORN EARWORM	Sweet corn Tomatoes	Inject ½ medicine dropperful of mineral oil into silk channel as silks start to dry. An early spraying of *Bacillus thuringiensis* (Bt) will help if the worms have not entered the ear.	
STRIPED CUCUMBER BEETLE	Cucumbers Melons Squash	Spray with rotenone or pyrethrum as soon as beetles appear.	For small plantings, cover the area with fine mesh or cheesecloth. Clean up crop debris. Soldier beetles prey on these.
CUTWORM	Most garden crops	A spray of *Bacillus thuringiensis* (Bt) will help after dark. Cutworms hide in the soil during the day.	At transplanting, wrap stems of seedling cabbage, pepper, and tomato plants with newspaper or foil to prevent damage by cutworms. They cut small plants off at ground level.

Insect	Crop	Spray Formula	Remarks
FLEA BEETLE	Most garden crops	Garlic and hot pepper sprays. Rotenone spray. Pyrethrum spray.	Injury is first noticed as tiny holes in foliage.
GRASSHOPPER	Most garden crops	Ryania or sabadilla spray.	Treat infested areas while grasshoppers are still small.
HORNWORM	Tomatoes	Spray with *Bacillus thuringiensis* (Bt).	Hand-picking is ordinarily more practical in the home garden.
LEAFHOPPER	Beans Carrots Potatoes Cucumbers Muskmelons	Spray with a rotenone/pyrethrum blend or sabadilla.	Apply when plants are small. Apply to underside of foliage.
MEXICAN BEAN BEETLE	Beans	Spray with rotenone or pyrethrum.	Looks like a big ladybug. Pick by hand. Crush eggs and larvae.
POTATO BEETLE	Potatoes Eggplant Tomatoes	Spray with rotenone or sabadilla.	Pick by hand. Crush eggs on back of leaves.
SLUGS	Almost any leafy plant, and crops like zucchini and tomatoes	No spray.	Hand-pick or sprinkle with salt. Attract with boards, rocks, or sections of hose and then destroy. Trap and drown by setting out shallow pans of beer. Sprinkle wood ashes around plants. Keep grass mowed.
SQUASH BUG	Squash	Pyrethrum/rotenone blend.	Adults and brown egg masses can be hand-picked. Trap adults under shingles beneath plants. Kill young bugs soon after they hatch.
SQUASH VINE BORER	Squash	A pyrethrum spray will work if applied early in the season when the moth is around.	Look for wilted vines. Cut open vines to find borers. Remove and destroy plants if badly infested. Cover vines you have cut open with earth to encourage new roots to form.

poison curare is a botanical, too, but it is used by South American Indians to bring down large mammals. Treat rotenone and pyrethrum with respect, and follow label directions carefully. These organic controls do, however, offer the advantage of a shorter active lifespan than synthetic pesticides.

Dormant Oil and Insecticidal Soaps

Dormant oil is used early in the spring on fruit trees to smother egg cases. Insecticidal soaps are a form of fatty acid that appear to work by penetrating the pests' body membranes and causing body fluids to drain away. They work on aphids, mealybugs, whiteflies, earwigs, spider mites, and others, but do not seem to harm ladybugs.

A close inspection of your garden, particularly at night, may well reveal that most of the damage has been done by just one or two types of bugs. Once you've identified them, you can choose your action to match.

Animal Pest Control

Gardeners are by nature normally peace-loving, friendly, and kind folks. But when their treasured gardens are attacked by animal pests an

amazing change sometimes takes place and they seem capable of unleashing a full-scale war.

The good news is that many gardeners live in areas where animal pests are rarely a problem. But even in the city you can find an amazing array of wildlife, beginning with squirrels. Many new suburban developments have spread over the habitats of wildlife, so you may find some around.

When you do see animal damage, act quickly. A family of woodchucks can devastate an unprotected garden in just a few days.

Fence Defense

A well-designed fence is the best defense. It can be expensive, but it can also save your garden. Once built, it needs only to be maintained from year to year. We have acres of land in garden and live in the country surrounded by acres of woods, so I have tried just about every kind of fence.

My favorite is made of 3-foot-high chicken wire with 1-inch or 1½-inch mesh, topped by a single strand of electric wire set 1 inch above the top. If you grow corn, an electric fence is the only sure way to keep raccoons out. If you want to take a chance, forget the electric wire and surround your corn with plantings of

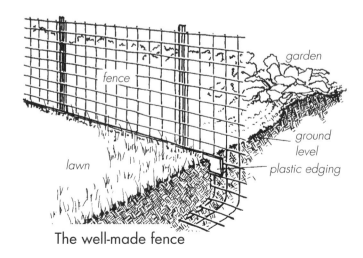

The well-made fence

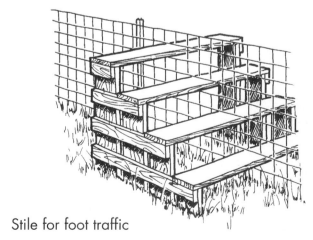

Stile for foot traffic

pumpkins and squash. Raccoons don't like to walk across these plants, which have a prickly, hairy feel. With an electric fence, you only need to power it up (usually by battery) during the corn harvest period. Normally, raccoons know just how to pick the ears of corn the day before you would harvest them for your table.

Big gardens need big gates—at least 5 feet wide to get carts, tillers, and other equipment in and out. Be sure to leave enough room around the edges of the garden to turn your tiller around . . . about 5 feet from fence to garden edge.

It's easy to estimate how much fence you'll need. Just measure your garden and expand it by 5 feet for turning room. For example, to construct an electric fence 10 feet all around a 30' x 40' garden, you'd need:

    180 feet of 3-foot-high chicken wire
    1 box of porcelain or plastic insulators
    180 feet of 12-gauge electric wire
    1 "fencer" to boost battery voltage
    1 six-volt "hot-shot" battery
    20 posts
    1 gate handle
    1 set of gate hinges

Home Remedies

One of the most interesting gardening pastimes is listening to gardeners who have tried various folk remedies to ward off pests. Many of these do work, but they may not work consistently.

🐛 Havahart traps. One friend of mine has had excellent luck by building a lightweight, temporary fence around the garden at the first sign of damage. He leaves a hole just wide enough for the trap, and catches woodchucks, skunks, and even raccoons as they

If your garden is near a wooded area, you'll probably have to build a strong fence with an electric wire on it to keep out raccoons, squirrels, and other four-legged marauders.

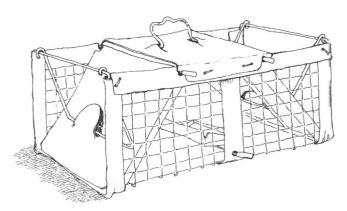

Consider a humane (Havahart) trap for the small animals that are raiding your garden. You can release your captives somewhere where they won't get into trouble.

enter through the "gate." Sometimes you can actually see paths in the grass where woodchucks head for your garden, and it is best to set your trap on one of these "game trails." You can move a skunk in a Havahart trap without getting sprayed by covering it with a blanket first. You can even drive them away in a car, covered up. Release the gate with a hoe, and make

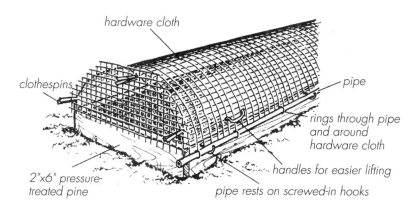

hardware cloth

clothespins

pipe

rings through pipe
and around
hardware cloth

2"x6" pressure-
treated pine

handles for easier lifting

pipe rests on screwed-in hooks

A nibble-proof raised bed.

sure the skunk has a clear route of escape. No sudden moves, please!

☙ Human hair, hung in cloth bags around the edges of the garden, repels deer. Hanging strongly scented soap also deters them.

☙ A gopher snake sent down a gopher hole is a good cure.

☙ Small portable radios protected by plastic bags keep after-dark pests away if allowed to play all night.

☙ Dried blood keeps away rabbits and woodchucks (and provides plants with nitrogen), but it washes into the ground with each rain and must be reapplied often.

☙ Black pepper sprinkled on plants makes rabbits sneeze and move along.

☙ Hot pepper and garlic sprays like those used for bugs may also deter pests.

☙ Dogs scare away animal pests, and one friend found that his pest problems ended for several years when a fox moved into the meadow near his garden.

CHAPTER 12

HARVESTING
THE FRUITS OF YOUR LABOR

THE HOME GARDENER has an advantage over the commercial vegetable grower; he does not have to harvest his crops before they are ripe. The commercial grower has to plan ahead so that his produce will ripen as it reaches the market. You can pick your vegetables just as they reach their prime.

Knowing when vegetables are perfect for picking is a skill that you will gain with experience. In general, though, it is best to bring things in from the garden just before you are going to eat them or prepare them for storage in the freezer, in a root cellar, or in canning jars. With every minute that passes from the time the produce is picked until the time it is eaten or processed, the vegetables lose quality and food value. Never leave fresh vegetables sitting around for a long time. If, for some reason, you have to pick vegetables a while before they are going to be used, keep them either in the refrigerator or in a cool, dark cellar. This will slow down the deterioration process.

Tomatoes are ready for harvest when they are deep red and come off the vine with just a gentle twist and pull.

Peas are ready to harvest when you can feel a good-sized pea inside if you squeeze the pod gently. Open a few pods just to be sure.

Carrots are very tasty if they are pulled when they get to be the size of your little finger. This is the best size to freeze, and pulling these baby carrots will make room for their neighbors to expand. Look for the darkest greens in the carrot patch to find the most mature carrots.

Harvest summer squash at all these stages of development. You can harvest the tiny ones while the blossom still clings to the plant. Try them in stir-fries. The plant will keep producing, so don't be afraid to harvest the small squash.

You can begin harvesting potatoes as soon as the plant produces its white blossoms, but you'll get a bigger harvest if you wait until fall when the plants die back.

Some vegetables can be picked before they are completely mature. Young onions, beets, carrots, cabbages, and the leaves from head lettuce plants that have not had time to form heads are all delicious. I think you will find that most of the early crops in your garden will mature quite suddenly, and that there is an all-too-short period of time to harvest them before they go by. Later varieties and succession crops are not so frustrating, because they ripen in the fall when the weather is cooler and, because it *is* cooler, they are not apt to mature quite so quickly.

If you want your plants to continue to bear vegetables, you must keep them harvested. Pick everything you can as soon as it is ready, even if you know that it is impossible for you to use it all. If you have to, throw your surplus on the compost pile. Putting unused vegetables back into the garden soil is not nearly so wasteful as throwing them away. Better still, make plans to preserve some of what you have left over, or share some with friends, neighbors, and needy folks. Giving fresh vegetables away is one of the friendliest gestures I know.

The crops you harvest latest in the season

YIELDS FOR PROCESSING

AVERAGE YIELD 100-FOOT ROW

Vegetables	16-Inch Wide Row	Single-Row Planting	Amount Fresh Needed Per Quart	Quarts Processed from One Bushel
BEETS	4 bu.	2 bu. (104 lbs.)	2½ lbs.	16-20 qts.
CARROTS	5 bu.	2 bu. (100 lbs.)	2½ lbs.	16-20 qts.
CORN	—	6 dozen ears	6-10 ears	6-8 qts.
GREENS	8 bu.	3 bu. (54 lbs.)	3 lbs.	4-8 qts.
OKRA	—	1,000 pods	2 lbs.	15-18 qts.
PEAS	4 bu.	2 bu. in pods (60 lbs.)	4 lbs.	8-10 qts.
SHELL AND LIMA BEANS	4 bu.	2 bu. in pods (60 lbs.)	4 lbs.	8-10 qts.
SNAP BEANS	4 bu.	2 bu. in pods (60 lbs.)	4 lbs.	8-10 qts.
SOUTHERN PEAS	4 bu.	2 bu. in pods (60 lbs.)	4 lbs.	8-10 qts.
SQUASH	—	135 squash	4 lbs.	10-12 qts.
TOMATOES	—	3 bu. (160 lbs.)	3 lbs.	15-18 qts.

are the easiest and best ones to store. Your root cellar—if you have one—will have cooled off by this time. Potatoes, cabbages, and turnips should be ready just in time to go into the root cellar. Eat your first plantings of beets and carrots throughout the summer months, and plan to use your later plantings for canning and freezing.

People often boast about having the biggest beets or carrots. This is fine for your ego, or if you want something to take to the fair, but eating these things is sometimes like chewing on a piece of old shoe leather. I like to grow vegetables that I call "table size." This means harvesting beets, for example, when they are slightly larger than a lemon. Carrots shouldn't be much bigger around than your thumb. Big, big vegetables have "gone by"; they have passed the point of being ripe, tender, and flavorful.

The more you harvest, the more you grow. It is very simple. If you don't pick your let-

These little cukes will be very tender and tasty. Large cucumbers tend to have tough seeds.

Beets are best harvested before they get to be big and old. Anything larger than a golf ball is a good eating size and fine to take.

Spinach, lettuce, and Swiss chard will keep producing new leaves for harvest if you cut the plants about 1 inch above the ground instead of pulling them up. This is called "cut and come again" harvesting.

tuce, it will go to seed. If you can't use all you have grown, give some to a friend. You will probably find that you can cut down the plants about three times before the lettuce gets bitter. Chard and other heat-tolerant greens can be cut continuously all summer long. If you keep cutting spinach, you can get as many as four harvests. Don't forget to cut little leaves, big leaves—the whole works.

All too often, when folks harvest leaf let-

tuce, they just pick at it. They take off one leaf at a time, picking only the biggest ones. What you should do is take a long knife or scissors and cut the whole row down to a height of about 1 inch. Don't cut down more than you can use at any one time. Keep moving down the row, cutting the lettuce as you need it. By the time you get to the end of the row, you can go back to the beginning and start all over again on the new lettuce that will have grown back.

This works just as well with chard. If you only pick the outer leaves, as many people do, you never get at the really good chard because you keep eating the older, tougher leaves. If you cut back the whole row, the little leaves will add to the tenderness and flavor of your crop, and the plants will continue to grow new leaves all season long.

People just pick at spinach in the same way. It's too bad that more folks don't cut it down. If you let spinach get 3 or 4 inches high and then cut down the whole row to a height of 1 inch, you can cut it several more times before it "bolts" and goes to seed. If you just pick away at it, one leaf at a time, you won't harvest much. A single 100-foot row of spinach can yield as little as two or three bags; by the time you cook it, you may wind up with only a quart or two. But if you plant a 10-inch-wide row, or even a 14-inch row, that is 100 feet long, I guarantee that you are going to get lots and lots of spinach—more than enough to give away.

Prolonging the Harvest Is Important

I believe in planting early to extend the growing season as much as possible. An old gentleman once told me that if I didn't lose at least some of my first or last crops, I wasn't

Broccoli plants produce one large head first. After it is cut the plant will produce many little heads. Yellow flowers on your broccoli means it has gone too far. Cut them off and discard them. More small heads will form.

planting early enough and wasn't trying to stretch out the season enough. Plant all of your hardiest crops as soon as the soil can be worked in the spring and again later in the summer for a fall crop.

There are two other ways to prolong your garden's productive period. One is to make several successive plantings of the same vegetable in different parts of the garden. The other method is to sow two or three varieties of the same crop—an early, a midseason, and a late variety.

You might, for example, plant three different varieties of sweet corn. You will find growing times listed on seed packets or in your favorite catalog. If you choose the right combination of varieties, you can have a second crop ripening at just about the time you have finished harvesting the first. If you sow bush beans and pole beans at the same time, your bush beans will have stopped producing by the time the pole beans are ready.

Believe it or not, a program for a long harvest period begins sometime in the middle of winter, when you should be carefully reading and studying the maturation times of the

You can tell when an ear of corn is mature without peeling it back. Immature ears will have a sharp point, but mature ears will be filled out and feel more flat at the top. With a little practice you'll never miss.

Don't pull out the whole cabbage plant when you harvest the first head. Cut off the head when it is small and tender, leaving three or four leaves. Small heads form for later harvest at each leaf.

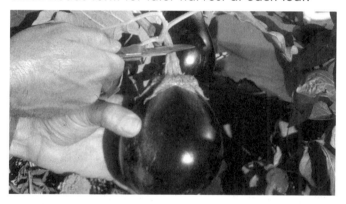

Eggplant should be harvested when it is dark purple and shiny. As it loses its shine it starts to get too old to be tender and tasty.

When onions are ready for harvest, their stalks will let you know by falling over. Harvest within ten days or the onions will not store well. You can also pull young onions up for use as scallions as soon as your seeds or sets send up healthy stalks.

vegetables you want to plant. If you know the number of days to maturity, you can accurately stagger the harvesting times by selecting the right varieties and by making successive plantings at strategic times.

Lettuce, cabbage, Brussels sprouts, beets, turnips, broccoli, carrots, chard, and rutabagas will continue to grow even after a frost. But, as fall approaches, get into the habit of listening closely to the weather forecasts on the radio and TV. Most tender plants can be protected from frost—at least for a while. It is a shame to let the very first frost of the season kill most of your garden. Many times, there will not be a second frost until weeks later.

Protecting tender plants like tomatoes, eggplant, peppers, cucumbers, and beans can add several weeks to your gardening season. Cover them with whatever you can find—old sheets and towels, polyethylene, old burlap bags, and any number of other things. The idea is just to keep them from being nipped by the frost. There is no need to try to keep the soil from freezing. It will stay warm enough by itself.

Later, when there is frost nearly every morning, you can bring some plants inside to grow a little longer in a warm window. This is a good time to cut "slips" from your tomato plants. Cut off a small sucker and put it in a glass of water. It will start to root in a day or so, and, when it does, you can plant it in a pot. Use the smaller varieties, such as Pixies and cherry tomatoes, unless you have lots of room inside.

Don't leave unripe tomatoes outside to freeze and rot. Bring them in while they are still green. Pull up the whole plant if you like. I have done this with peppers as well as tomatoes. I just hang the plant bottom-side-up in a dark room. Sooner or later, the fruit will ripen.

USING AND PRESERVING COMMON VEGETABLES

Vegetable	Salads	Cooking	Canning	Freezing	Storing	Other Remarks
BEANS	✓	✓	✓	✓	✓	Dried beans store well for winter use.
BEETS	1	✓	✓	✓	✓	Will store through winter in a box of moist sand in a cool basement.
BROCCOLI	✓	✓	—	✓	—	Plants grow one main head, and side shoots grow smaller heads.
BRUSSELS SPROUTS	—	✓	—	✓	—	Best grown as a fall crop. Harvest lasts well into winter.
CABBAGE	✓	✓	—	✓	2	Makes good sauerkraut for freezing.
CARROTS	✓	✓	✓	✓	✓	Will store through winter in a box of moist sand in a cool basement.
CAULIFLOWER	✓	✓	✓	✓	—	Best grown as a fall crop.
CHARD	✓	✓	✓	✓	—	Very hardy. Harvest can last into winter months.
CUCUMBERS	✓	—	✓	—	—	Especially good as pickles.
GREEN ONIONS	✓	—	—	✓	—	Dried onions will keep during winter in a cool, dry place.
LEEKS	—	✓	—	—	✓	Will store through winter in a box of moist sand in a cool basement.
PARSLEY	✓	✓	—	✓	—	Used mostly as garnish and seasoning.
PEAS	3	✓	✓	✓	—	Edible-podded peas are also good to grow for fresh use or in stir-fries.
PEPPERS	✓	✓	✓	✓	—	Especially good stuffed with meat or rice.
RADISH	✓	✓	—	—	—	Can be braised and served as a cooked vegetable.
SPINACH	✓	✓	✓	✓	—	Grows quickly during the cool weather of spring and fall.
TOMATOES	✓	✓	✓	✓	—	Green tomatoes picked before frost will ripen indoors during winter.
ZUCCHINI SQUASH	✓	✓	✓	✓	—	Can be used as a substitute for cucumbers in salads.

1 - Beets can be used in salads if cooked or pickled first.

2 - Some late-season varieties of cabbage store well.

3 - Edible-podded varieties of peas are suitable for salad use.

CHAPTER 13
GARDENING
WITH HERBS

HERBS ARE A GREAT CHOICE for a beginning gardener because they grow like weeds. Most of them are just that— weeds that come from all over the world. What makes them special are the volatile oils they contain that give them good flavor. Over the past few years interest in herbs has grown considerably, as more and more people have become interested in international cooking. Tarragon is a basic in many French recipes. Many Italian dishes get their distinctive flavor from oregano. Cilantro (coriander leaf) is found in some salsas, and is a prominent ingredient in Chinese and Thai cuisines.

Not only are herbs easy to grow, but there are lots of interesting things to do with them. Use them fresh, of course. But you can make those expensive herb vinegars you find in gourmet stores. You can also make herb butters, herb teas, and fresh herb salad dressings. Some people even put angelica, mint, rosemary, or thyme into their hot bath water, but I've never tried it myself.

Of course, the best reason to grow herbs is to get the fresh flavor that you'll never experience any other way. I'm no gourmet cook, but believe me, a sprig of dill or tarragon pressed against chicken or fish on the outdoor grill is a real treat. The same thing is true of rosemary on pork or lamb chops.

The Basics

Like other flowers and vegetables, herbs are either annuals that have to be started fresh every year, perennials that come back year after year, or biennial herbs—caraway and parsley, for instance—that grow for two years and then have to be replaced. (See the chart on page 112.) If you live in a very cold climate, you might find that some perennials behave like annuals and you have to start them fresh every year. But even up here in northern Vermont, herbs like chives, tarragon, mint, and oregano come back year after year. And dill tends to reseed itself and come back the following year whether you want it to or not. A few inches of mulch on your perennial herb bed in the

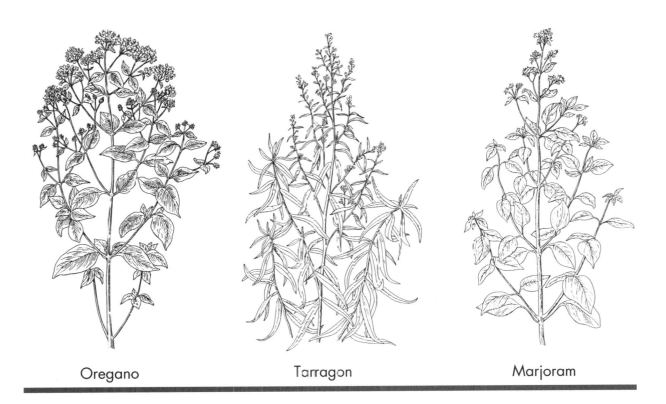

Oregano   Tarragon   Marjoram

fall can help carry it through the winter.

Garlic is also considered an herb. The serious cook will also want to grow shallots, which are a dividing onion often found in herb gardens. The supermarket is a good source of garlic and shallot bulbs if your garden store doesn't have them. You plant them just like onion sets. The bulb divides underground and you get six or eight in a cluster for each one that you plant.

Getting Started

You can probably find most of the basic herbs you want already started as transplants at your garden center. If you want to start your own, follow the directions in Chapter 5 for starting seeds with just a few changes. First, herb seeds usually are tiny. After leveling off your soil mix, sprinkle the herb seeds on the surface and just tamp them down. You don't have to bury

the tiny ones. Be sure to keep them moist and in a warm spot. The other big difference is that they seem to take forever to germinate and show themselves. Two or three weeks is not uncommon.

Another way to get perennial herbs like chives, oregano, and tarragon is to divide an existing plant. In early spring, or after the growing season in fall, drive a trowel or spade through the plant and remove a chunk for your garden. Be sure to keep the roots moist as you move them, and transplant them immediately.

Herbs Grow Almost Anywhere

You can grow a good collection of the basic herbs in one or two hanging baskets, in a small corner of your vegetable garden, in pots or window boxes, or even mixed in a flower bed. Potted herbs on a sunny kitchen windowsill will give you a fresh supply year-round. Plan ahead for perennials that will be back again next year.

Like most vegetables, herbs like five to eight hours of sunshine every day and soil that is rich in organic matter. Soil should be well drained, except for mint, which likes damp, partly shady areas.

My advice is to put your herbs as close to the kitchen as you can, because you'll use them a lot more if you don't have to make a special trip to the backyard garden for a few leaves of basil or chives.

The Top Ten

There are so many herbs available that it is easy to be bewildered by the choices. Grow a few and get to know what suits your taste and what you'll use the most. My choices for the five most used would be basil, chives, dill, oregano, and parsley. The next five would be French (not Russian) tarragon, marjoram,

mint, sage, and thyme. French tarragon, which is the kind you want for cooking, rarely sets seeds, and new plants come from either root cuttings, stem cuttings, or plant division. Avoid buying tarragon seeds: they're probably the Russian variety.

Planting

Set annual herbs out, just like vegetables, after all danger of frost has past. See the chart on page 112 for heights. The most unwieldy herb is dill, which gets so tall and rangy that you may have to stake it so it doesn't blow over.

Three or four plants will be enough for a family. If you plan to make pesto sauce, plant more basil, because most recipes start with 2 cups of pressed basil leaves, and that's a lot of leaves. If you plan to make dill pickles, be sure to put in more dill.

Care during the Growing Season

If you have fertilized the soil at planting time you shouldn't need more fertilizer during the growing season. Too much fertilizing will make herbs big and rangy, when what you're really after is compact bushy plants with greater concentrations of the flavorful oils.

Most herbs are at their best just as they begin to flower. This is the time to pick the tender leaves and pick off the flowers to encourage continued growth. Like vegetables, herbs will grow best if they are not allowed to set seeds. Prune them to control their size and shape as you harvest for your own use.

Tips on Using Herbs

Chives should be cut just above the ground and can be harvested three times during the

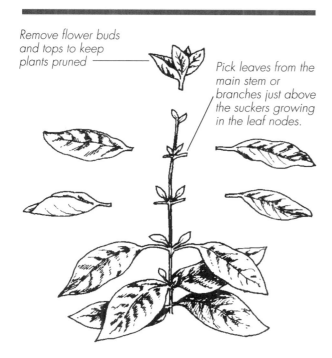

Remove flower buds and tops to keep plants pruned

Pick leaves from the main stem or branches just above the suckers growing in the leaf nodes.

Prune your basil plants for prolonged growth.

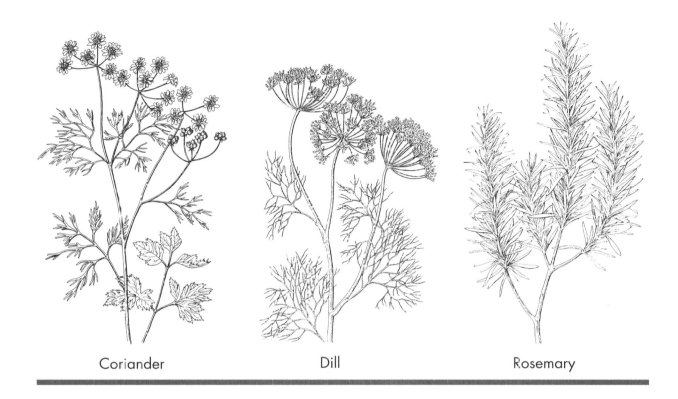

Coriander   Dill   Rosemary

season. Whenever you cut, be sure to leave some growth remaining to nourish the plant.

Basil can be harvested a few leaves or branches at a time as you need them, or you can cut the entire plant 6 to 8 inches above the ground, leaving one vigorous branch of old growth remaining to encourage a small second harvest.

Fresh herbs are not as strong as dried. As a rule of thumb, use 1 tablespoon of fresh herbs for every teaspoon of dried herbs called for in recipes.

Herbs will do the best job of flavoring if they are added to dishes late in the cooking—within 30 minutes of serving.

Some herbs are better frozen than dried. Just clean and pat the herbs dry with a paper towel, then pack them in plastic bags and quick-freeze them. Basil and chives can be either frozen or dried, but hold their flavor best if frozen. Dill, tarragon, marjoram, and mint can be dried and stored in airtight containers. Others can be dried or frozen.

Rosemary and parsley can be moved indoors for the winter. This is particularly important for rosemary in cold climates, where it won't winter over. Our rosemary just moves in and out of the house in a pot. Check for insects and rinse off any that you find.

Chamomile is not one of the most common herbs, but the small flowers are used in herb teas and as a rinse for blonde hair. Sown thickly and kept cut, chamomile can be used as a groundcover or turf.

In addition to sweet basil, try growing purple (or "opal leaf") basil for color in the garden or for making interesting basil vinegars. It is used just like green basil, but is not quite as sweet.

Herbs for immediate use will be tastier if harvested in the morning, before the sun has dried out the foliage.

FAVORITE COOKING HERBS

Herb	Grow from	Full height	Harvest, favorite uses
Annual Herbs *			
ANISE	Seed, transplant	24"	Clip leaves when the plants flower. Use leaves in salad; seeds for cookies, pastry.
BASIL	Seed, transplant	20-24"	Use leaves in soups, stews, salads, and sauces, including pesto. Good with tomato, fish, and egg dishes. Tip: Slice fresh tomatoes. Top with mozzarella cheese slices, snipped basil, wine vinegar, and olive oil for summer salad.
BORAGE	Seed, transplant	24"	Pick young leaves when plant is in flower. Use leaves in salad or cooked like spinach. Cucumberish flavor. Good in fish sauces. Tip: Don't bother drying; flavor vanishes unless fresh.
CORIANDER	Seed, transplant	36"	Cut stalks when seeds ripen. Crush seeds to use in meat sauces, pickles, pastry, bread. Fresh leaves (known as cilantro) used in salsa, on top of roasts, in pea or chicken soups, and in oriental cuisines.
DILL	Seed, transplant	24-36"	Use seeds and foliage fresh or dried. Snip young green seeds and leaves into salad. Dried seed heads in pickles. Sprig of fresh foliage perks up sandwiches; flavors fish on the grill and steamed vegetables, especially carrots.
SAVORY (Summer)	Seed, transplant	18"	Harvest shoots as the plants flower. Use leaves fresh or dried with meats, fish, soups, beans.
Biennial Herbs			
CARAWAY	Seed, transplant	12-24"	Use leaves in salad, seeds in breads, soups, sauerkraut. Tip: Seeds are good on fresh steamed carrots, with butter or sauce. Cut seed heads before dry.
PARSLEY	Seed, transplant	6-12"	Use fresh in salads, soups, stews. Substitute for basil in pesto sauce. Tip: Bring indoors in a pot for winter use.
Perennial Herbs			
CHIVES	Seed, or divide an established plant	8-12"	Mild onion flavor best known as topping with sour cream on baked potato. Snip into salads, soups, sauces, eggs. Mix with cream cheese.

Herb	Grow from	Full height	Harvest, favorite uses
MARJORAM	Seed, transplant— many varieties	12"	Use fresh or dried leaves in salad, soup, stuffings.
MINT	Divide or transplant; likes moist areas.	13"	Leaves used in iced tea, lemonade. Good with lamb, or snipped into peas, carrots. Tip: Mint spreads via underground runners and will take over. Try growing in containers or enclosures. Used dried mint, chopped in a blender, as a stomach-soothing tea.
OREGANO	Seed, transplant, or division	24"	Cut tips. Used in many Italian dishes, soups, roasts, stews, and salads. Tip: Oregano is easily confused with marjoram. Crush a leaf and smell it to be sure.
ROSEMARY	Seed, stem cuttings, transplant	36"	Cut pine-needle–like leaves before flowering. Good with pork or lamb as seasoning during cooking.
SAGE	Seed, stem cuttings, transplant	18"	Leaves used sparingly with fatty meats like sausage, pork, duck. Used in cheeses and chowders. Dry carefully; tends to mold. Fresh is much better than dried. Tip: Mix a few fresh chopped leaves with cottage cheese.
TARRAGON	Plant division, or buy plants of French, not Russian, tarragon	24"	Use tender leaves in salad and on fish or chicken during grilling. Use with eggs, mushrooms. Tip: Make tarragon vinegar like sun tea, using white wine vinegar and 2-3 tops of tarragon stalks per wine bottle.
THYME	Seed, transplant,	8-12"	Pick leaves when flowers open. Basic in soup stock and used sparingly on mutton, veal, pork, rabbit, and chicken. Snip into salads.

Mint will form runners which will root as shown. These runners can be cut apart, and the new small plants can be transplanted. Beware, however, because mint is invasive and will take over an entire bed in a few years if not confined.

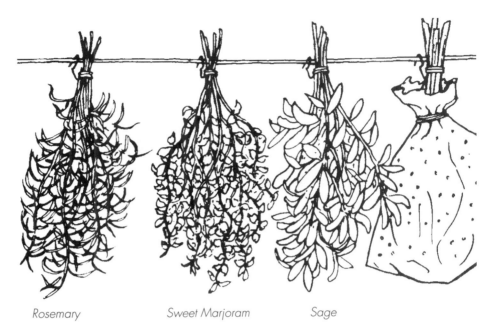

Rosemary   Sweet Marjoram   Sage

Tie freshly picked herbs in small bunches and hang them upside down to dry in a dark airy place. Some people place the bundles in paper bags with air holes punched in them to reduce exposure to light and dust.

Harvesting and Drying Herbs

Rosemary and thyme can be cut at full bloom, but most other herbs should be harvested just before the flowers open.

Drying is simple. Cut the herb off near the ground and pick off any unhealthy looking leaves. Wash and pat dry. Tie the stalks together and hang them upside down in a well-ventilated, dust-free room. I punch several holes in brown paper bags and hang the herbs upside down inside the bags. This allows air to circulate but keeps them clean and out of light that might dilute their flavor. Once dry, put them in airtight glass jars and label them. To chop, remove thick stems and run them through a blender. Small amounts can be chopped using a coffee grinder.

Some Simple Recipes for Herbs

Herb butters can be used on bread, toast, baked potatoes, and vegetables or tossed with pasta. One tablespoon minced fresh herb is stirred into ¼ cup of soft butter. Refrigerate the herb butter overnight to let the flavors blend before using it. Try dill or basil first, then experiment with other herbs.

Pesto sauce is usually used on pasta, but it also goes well with baked potatoes, broiled fish, or fresh vegetables as a dip. The basic pesto recipe is:

> *2 cups firmly packed fresh basil leaves*
> *¼ cup pine nuts or walnuts*
> *3 cloves garlic, peeled*
> *¾ cup freshly grated Parmesan cheese*
> *¼ cup olive oil*

Add the oil slowly after blending the other ingredients in a blender or food processor. If you're going to freeze large amounts, hold out the garlic and crush it in before serving the pesto to preserve the garlic flavor.

A basic fresh herb salad dressing is:

6 tablespoons oil
3 tablespoons vinegar
¼ teaspoon salt
¼ teaspoon dry mustard
Freshly ground pepper to taste
1 to 2 cloves garlic, peeled and pressed
2 to 3 tablespoons fresh herbs

(Try using basil, dill, marjoram, oregano, sage, tarragon, or thyme, either alone or in combinations, until you hit upon your favorite blend.)

Herb vinegars are expensive to buy but easy to make, and once you know the basics you can experiment with endless combinations. White wine vinegar is usually used, but I prefer cider vinegar. Put 1 cup of chopped or crushed herbs in a glass jar and pour a quart of vinegar over them. One or two cloves of garlic and a few peppercorns are optional. Put the jar in a warm, sunny place for a few days, then strain into another bottle or several smaller bottles. Add a sprig of fresh herbs to each bottle, seal with a cork, and store in a cool, dark place. Avoid using metal lids, strainers, or spoons when making vinegar.

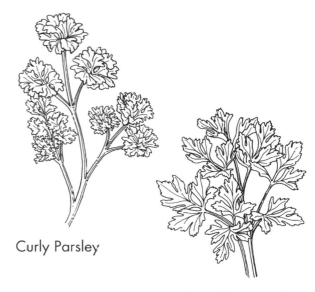

Curly Parsley

Flat (Italian) Parsley

CHAPTER 14

CULTURAL
INFORMATION FOR EACH VEGETABLE

ACH VEGETABLE HAS its own personality and its own particular likes and dislikes. Seed catalogs usually provide the most complete information on growing the specific varieties of vegetables that you purchase for planting in your garden. As I suggested earlier, you'll probably want to get several seed catalogs from different companies, not only to check out the different varieties they offer, but to compare information that will help you plan your garden.

The following alphabetical roundup of some favorite fruits, vegetables, and herbs provides some crucial growing information that you may or may not find in seed catalogs. It will help you in planning, to be sure, but it will also introduce you to some of the tips and techniques that I've discovered or developed over the years through my own gardening activities. The information in these entries isn't meant to be exhaustive, though, and you should use it in conjunction with the growing instructions found on seed packets and in

catalog listings.

Make a photocopy of the customized planning chart on pp.176-183 to use in recording which varieties you plant, as well as other dates and details about your gardening year. This chart contains some of the growing information found in this chapter, such as planting and thinning distances. Keep old charts on hand, even after the growing season is over: they'll prove invaluable in planning future gardens.

Asparagus

Asparagus is a perennial, which means that it will come back year after year. A perennial bed must stay in the same place for a long time, so give careful thought to its location. Once an asparagus patch is established, it is very difficult to work the soil there very thoroughly. Be sure to add all the humus, manure, and organic matter you can when you prepare the bed, because the plants may be there for 20 years or more.

Asparagus is only harvested in the spring when the young shoots come up. In the summer and fall, the ferns must be allowed to grow very tall as they go to seed. The seeds come in lovely, bright red berries, and the feathery ferns make a fine hedge. But be careful not to put the bed in a spot where the ferns will shade shorter garden plants.

You can raise asparagus from seed, but it is better to buy roots that are one or two years old. You will get asparagus much more quickly this way. Asparagus grows in most types of soil, but it does best in sandy loam. Drainage is important; asparagus cannot survive in water-logged earth. An annual application of fertilizer will keep the bed in good condition. I recommend about 10 pounds of 10–10–10 fertilizer for every 200 square feet.

If you live in the North, set out asparagus roots in the early spring. In the South, they should be set out in the fall. Plants should be spaced about 1 foot apart, with 4 feet between rows. A 100-foot row is enough to feed a family of four.

Planting asparagus takes a bit of work, but it is worth doing right. You won't have to do it again for 20 or 30 years if you take care of the bed properly. Dig a trench about a foot deep and about a foot and a half wide. In the bottom of this trench, make little mounds of earth combined with compost, manure, or fertilizer. Space them about 1 foot apart. Make the mounds tall enough to place the "crown" of the plant, the point where the roots converge, about 3 inches below the top of the trench. Drape the roots, like a skirt, over the mound. Once all the crowns are positioned properly, fill in the trench and firm the soil. Each crown should be covered with about 3 inches of gently compacted soil.

A week or so after planting, rake the top of the bed to destroy whatever weeds may be growing there. Be careful not to cut or disturb the asparagus crowns. Some people like to mulch young asparagus with hay, leaves, or some other kind of organic matter. This is not a bad idea, but don't mulch until the asparagus is up and showing.

Expect no harvest at all the first year.

ASPARAGUS PLANTING INSTRUCTIONS

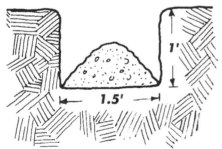 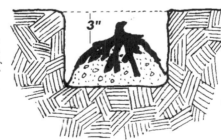 

Mound up a mix of soil and compost, manure, or fertilizer in the bottom of the planting trench. Space the mounds 1 foot apart.

Drape the asparagus roots over the mound, leaving the crown 3 inches below the top of the trench. Fill up the trench and firm the soil.

To extend the harvest, plant the crowns at different depths. The deepest plants will send up shoots last.

Leave the plants alone throughout the summer and fall; do not cut the ferns until the dead of winter. Better still, don't cut them down at all. Wait until spring. The ferns are very important to next year's crop of asparagus.

You can harvest very sparingly the second spring. Pick or cut shoots for a week or so, then allow the ferns to grow freely again. Harvest only those that are as big around as your thumb. The shoots are at their prime when they are 6 to 8 inches tall. If they are small and skinny, about the size of a pencil, leave them alone and let them grow. They will produce a crop for the following year. During the third spring, you can harvest liberally for four to six weeks. Normally, you can plan to harvest asparagus for five to ten weeks in an established bed, depending on your location.

I've discovered a few tricks that allow me to extend my harvesting time. I plant my asparagus at different levels. In one-third of my asparagus bed, I dig a deep, deep trench. Here I plant the crowns 6 or 7 inches below the surface. In the next third of the patch, I come up a couple of inches so that the crowns are about 4 or 5 inches beneath the surface. In the last third, I plant the crowns 2 or 3 inches deep.

In the spring, the plants that are closest to the surface send up shoots first. I get a very early harvest from these. Those that are a little deeper come along a little later, and those that have been planted 6 or 7 inches below the surface come up later still. I find that I can prolong the harvest for an extra three weeks this way.

You can accomplish the same thing with mulch. Lay about 4 inches of fairly heavy mulch over your entire bed. Leaves will work fine, especially if they are chopped. Early in the spring, pull the mulch away from about half of your patch. The asparagus will come up much more quickly where the soil has been laid bare. The mulched soil in the rest of the bed will stay cool longer, and this will hold back the growth of the asparagus. As soon as shoots begin to poke through the mulch, carefully rake it away. If you don't, the asparagus is apt to come up and then curl over.

Early in the spring, as soon as the ground starts to thaw, I go over the surface of the soil with a rototiller, being careful not to till more than an inch or so deep. This gets rid of a good share of the weeds, grinds up the old ferns, and adds organic matter to the soil. I find that this is one of the best times to fertilize because I can see what I am doing. If fertilizer is added in the fall, the nitrogen in the 10–10–10 seems to disappear into the soil and lasts no longer than about a month. Fertilizing in the spring helps to ensure a bountiful harvest.

Beans, Pole

The nicest thing about pole beans is that you can easily raise a lot of them in very little space. All you have to do is cut some poles about 8

HORTICULTURAL BEANS

Horticultural bean is the standard catalog name for a colorful, popular bean known by a number of aliases. These plump, attractive beans are best if shelled after the pods begin to turn slightly dry. (Southerners call beans used at this stage "shucky.") In other parts of the country, horticultural beans are called speckled cranberry beans or bird's-egg beans.

118

feet long, stick them in the ground about 3 feet apart, and plant five or six seeds in a circle around the base of each pole. The seeds should be 6 to 8 inches away from the pole itself.

As the plants begin to grow, they will send out tendrils which will wind themselves clockwise around the pole as they climb to the top. Be sure that poles are set firmly in the ground so they won't blow over in windy weather. Sometimes you will have to direct the bean tendrils toward the pole. They have been known to grow in the wrong direction —that is, away from the pole.

Pole beans really live up to their name. They will not interweave themselves through horizontal wires; they will only grow up poles or similar vertical objects. If you try to support the vines with horizontal strings or wires, they are likely to wind around each other and choke themselves out. You can, though, put a pole at either end of a row, run a wire from the top of one to the top of the other, and then run strings from this wire directly to the ground. Pole beans will grow on these, but they will not grow well on chicken wire or snow fence. Some folks hitch the tops of three poles together and spread out the bottoms so that they make a sort of tripod or teepee. Then they make plantings around the base of each pole. This is more than just an efficient way to use space; these teepees stand up well in the wind. I have also seen pole beans planted in with corn. The tendrils grow right up the cornstalks. Just plant one bean seed for every three kernels of corn.

The most popular variety of pole bean is Kentucky Wonder. Romano, a slightly wider Italian pole bean, is good too. They both have a slightly nutty taste—excellent flavor! Both are now also available as bush beans.

STAKING POLE BEANS

Fasten three bean stakes together at the top to form a tripod. Anchor tripods firmly so they don't blow over.

Another good way to stake beans is to place a pole where you will plant every other hill, then run a string, binders' twine, or wire along the bottoms and tops of the poles down the entire length of the row. Between the poles, tie a vertical string to the ground string. Plant a hill of beans at every pole and every vertical string. You'll find that a bean plant will climb up the string quicker than up the pole.

Beans, Bush

Beans are one of the easiest vegetables to grow. Every garden should include at least a few, because they return a lot of vegetable protein for very little effort. Beans will be ready for harvest 8 to 12 weeks after they are planted, depending on the variety. Unfortunately, you must not plant them until after all danger of frost has passed. They are not at all hardy.

Beans require very little fertilizer. As a matter of fact, they are what we call a "nitrogen-fixing legume." This means that they contribute more nitrogen to the soil than they take from it.

When you plant bush beans, be sure to leave plenty of room between rows, because the plants will grow quite wide. If you plant in a single row, the row will become at least a foot wide as the plants mature. Leave yourself enough room to walk, harvest, and cultivate between rows.

If you plant in wide rows, you will be able to grow about four times as many beans in the same garden space. Bean seeds should be planted 2½ to 3 inches apart, so if you lay out rows 10 to 14 inches wide, you should sprinkle three to five seeds across the row. With a little practice, you will be able to space the seeds evenly. You should have ripe beans anywhere from ten days to two weeks after the first blossoms appear.

For a big bean harvest, plant a pound of bean seeds in a block 10 feet by 10 feet square. This area will produce 50 pounds of beans. After the soil has been turned over, mix in 1 pound of organic fertilizer and the pound of bean seeds. Then either turn them in with a tiller or rake them into the ground. You can plant peas the same way.

There are two basic types of bush beans—green-podded snap beans and yellow-podded wax beans. Two excellent varieties of snap beans are Bountiful and Tendergreen. To get a continuous harvest of beans, you should make at least two plantings at two- to three-week intervals. Harvest them when they are just about the size of a pencil. Do not wait until large seeds start forming inside the pod, making the whole bean look lumpy. The most flavorful and nutritious beans are the young and tender ones. After your first picking, you can pick again in about three days. Beans grow very fast, and you can get several harvests from one planting as long as you keep them picked.

Once your bushes have finally stopped bearing, they should be tilled into the garden or pulled up and thrown on the compost pile. The bean-growing area can immediately be replanted with a fall crop, like beets or carrots. You must never weed, cultivate, handle, or harvest beans either when the weather is wet or right after a heavy dew. If you touch the leaves when they are damp, you may transmit disease organisms which will cause a rust or blight that can ruin the quality of the beans and even destroy the plant.

Beans, Lima

Lima bean plants are very bushy. They need even more distance between rows than regular bush beans—at least 3 feet. The seeds should be planted about 4 inches apart with about an inch and a half of firmed soil over them. They too can be planted in single rows or in wide bands. I personally like wide rows, because the plants hold each other up and keep the pods off the ground.

It takes 11 to 12 weeks for lima beans to reach maturity. Remember these dates when you plan your garden, and be sure that you have a long-enough growing season. In many northern areas, lima beans must be planted very early to produce any crop at all. You can gain a week or so by sprouting them indoors inside damp paper towels.

Lima beans like warm, well-drained soil and need little fertilizer. As is the case with most bean patches, stay out of the lima beans when they are wet. Lima beans are ready to be harvested when beans have formed inside the pods. The pods will look fat when the limas are ripe. You will find anywhere from two to five beans in each one, depending on the year and on how well they have grown. If your season is long enough, you can let them mature and then dry in the sun.

Pole Lima Beans

When grown in wet weather, bush lima beans pick up an unpleasant, earthy taste where the pods touch the ground. This is an advantage pole limas have over bush limas. Pole limas also have a better flavor and yield much better

---

BUTTER BEANS

Lima beans, picked when the bean is small and green and cooked in milk and butter, are called "butter beans" in the South. Many southerners use that name for all lima beans.

LIMA BEAN HONEY

The nectar that bees collect from lima bean blossoms makes one of the lightest-colored honeys—and one of the most delectable. Be careful not to spray with toxic insecticides when the beans are in bloom. If you need to spray, do so very late in the day when the bees are not working.

---

and longer than bush limas.

Pick pole lima beans heavily. As long as you keep enough moisture and fertilizer in the ground, the more you pick, the more they will produce. They produce to make seed, as do all plants, so if you leave a few beans on the plant, it is satisfied and quits bearing.

Be sure lima beans are filled out completely before picking. You should get 1 pound of shelled limas for every 2 pounds of beans in the pod.

Beets

Beets are very hardy and will grow in most kinds of soil. They can be planted in the spring as soon as the soil can be tilled; frost will injure neither the seed nor the young plants. Later in the year, other sowings can be made to provide beets for fall eating and storage.

Again, you can plant beets in single rows or in wide rows. Wide rows will yield a lot more for a lot less work. You should plant beet seeds about an inch deep and about 2 inches apart. Because they are slow to come up, I like to plant radishes in with beets to mark the rows. Every beet seed you plant may produce as many as six seedlings. When the tiny beet leaves poke through the soil, there may be four or five plants in a cluster. These must be thinned.

Cultivation is important, too. One of the first things I do is drag a regular garden rake gently across the row. This seems to make an awful mess, but it is an easy way to get the first cultivation and thinning done.

When the beets start to form little bulbs about the size of marbles, I pull out the largest ones and eat both the green tops and the small beets. This leaves room for the other roots to expand. I keep harvesting beet greens throughout the summer.

I try to keep the soil around beets as loose as possible. This is pretty easy for me because the soil in my garden is quite sandy. Raising beets and other root crops in heavy clay soil is another matter. But there are ways to solve the clay problem. The simplest answer is to dig a shallow trench or furrow and throw in a liberal amount of organic matter; leaves, manure, or compost will do just fine. Cover the organic matter with a small amount of soil and plant your seeds on top of it. The loose organic matter will not only provide lots of nutrients, it will also give the root crops some room to expand. Root crops also do well when grown in raised beds. Don't forget about using icicle radishes as a natural cultivator in clay soil.

The Detroit Dark Red beet is a wonderful winter keeper. For delicious greens and early eating, try the Early Wonder variety. Plant plenty of beets. You may want to make pickles or beet relish from the extras. Starting beets inside for later transplanting is a good way to have a crop before anyone else in the neighborhood.

Fortunately, insects don't trouble beets very much. They take care of themselves for the most part. You shouldn't have to worry about dusting or spraying.

Broccoli

Broccoli is a member of the cabbage family. All the members of this family should be treated in pretty much the same way. Start them inside in late April or early May. They can stand some frost, but not too much.

I like to have broccoli early in the year, so I start some seed indoors and transplant them outdoors when the seedlings have become small, healthy plants. Unfortunately, broccoli that is set out this way does not seem to be as good as broccoli grown from seed in the garden. You can also plant leaf lettuce in a wide row with broccoli. The lettuce will form a living mulch for the broccoli, and the broccoli will provide shade for the lettuce.

When I set out transplants, I space them at the recommended interval—16 inches apart in a 2–1–2 wide-row staggered planting. At the same time, I plant two broccoli seeds between each plant. Weeks later, when the transplanted broccoli starts to head, the new seedlings will be coming along quite well and will soon be forming heads of their own. This will be delicious late broccoli.

Broccoli plants grow fairly large, so they require 16 inches between plants and 3 feet between rows. They like a little fertilizer, so do them a favor and put a handful of manure or compost under each plant. If you prefer, you can mix a bit of 5–10–10 or organic fertilizer with the soil surrounding the roots.

Worms seem to think that broccoli is particularly tasty. When you transplant, be sure to wrap a collar of newspaper around the stem to keep cutworms away. Regular use of Bt should solve your problems with cabbage worms. (Incidentally, those white butterflies you see around your garden lay the eggs for cabbage worms.) Green cabbage worms may find their way into broccoli heads if you don't dust them once every three or four days.

A broccoli head is actually a cluster of many flower buds. This cluster should be harvested before the tiny yellow flowers begin to open. The first head may be as small as an apple or as large as 6 or 8 inches across. A few days after you have cut out the central cluster, smaller lateral heads will start to form on different parts of the stem. These will not be nearly as large as the first head, but they are just as good to eat.

The more you pick, the more heads your broccoli plants will produce. As soon as you allow them to blossom, they will stop trying to make those little flower buds which eventually produce seed. Harvest as often as every three days, and keep harvesting as long as there is something to pick.

For a fall crop of broccoli, you might start plants from seed right in the garden ten weeks before the first fall frost. The seeds should be planted 3 or 4 inches apart. In two or three weeks they should be about right for transplanting 16 inches apart in the 2–1–2 wide-row pattern. The best thing about late broccoli—aside from its great taste and its ability to withstand some frost—is that it is relatively worm-free. The natural worm cycles seem to occur in the spring and throughout the warm summer months.

It is always a good idea to rotate your crops. If you plant broccoli in one spot this year, don't plant broccoli—or any other member of the cabbage family, for that matter—in the same spot next year.

Brussels Sprouts

Some people like to start Brussels sprouts early to get a midsummer crop, but I see them as basically a fall vegetable. They sure taste better if you harvest them in the late fall. They will stand many, many freezes during September, October, and November. Here in Vermont, I have picked Brussels sprouts as late as January. I had to dig in the snow for them.

Space your transplants just as you would space broccoli—16 inches apart. The edible portion is the marble- to golf-ball–sized head that grows right on the stem. A sprout will form just above the point where a leaf grows out of the thick stalk. If you break off some of the lowest leaves, you can encourage early heads to form higher on the plant. I like to remove all the leaves on the bottom 6 inches of stalk. I do it in the morning when the dew is still on them and they snap off very easily.

Once I start harvesting, I take off another two or three layers of leaves, stripping the stalk 3 or 4 inches higher. I find that this stimulates very tall growth. The plants will grow 3 feet high if you fertilize them well and keep breaking off the lower leaves.

Bugs will bother Brussels sprouts in the same way that they bother cabbage. Usually they can be controlled with Bt.

The sprouts can be picked as soon as they are a little bigger than the end of your thumb. Sometimes two or three new sprouts will grow to replace each one you pick, as long as you don't cut them too close to the stem. Brussels sprouts are fun. Don't be afraid to experiment with them a little.

Cabbage

Cabbages will thrive in nearly any kind of soil. I have discovered that early cabbage does well in light soil, and that fall cabbages do best in heavy, damp soil.

Start your seedlings three to four weeks before you plan to set them out. You will see that they grow very fast. Harden them off, but don't worry too much about a late spring frost killing them. They are quite hardy and will survive a light freeze or two. Keep in mind that a handful of manure or compost under each plant will be a real asset to it. Cutworms can be a problem, so don't forget the newspaper-collar trick. Spacing is not so critical with cabbage plants. Leave from 15 to 18 inches between them, and they should do fine.

When you harvest early cabbage, cut off the head and leave the stem. If you are lucky, three or four smaller heads will grow to replace the first one. These small heads will be useful in recipes calling for small amounts of cabbage.

Your fall crop can be planted from seed 12 weeks before the first fall frost. When these seedlings get to be about 3 inches tall, transplant them in a 2–1–2 pattern, spaced 12 to 16 inches apart. For some reason, late cabbage tends to get larger than early cabbage.

Cabbage requires some fertilizer, but not much. If you feed it too much, the heads may burst. I used to be alarmed by this until I discovered a cure. Cabbage heads, like all vegetable heads, grow from the inside out. If you notice that yours are starting to crack, this probably means that the cabbages are growing so fast in the center that the outside growth cannot keep up. If you let this continue, the whole thing will break wide open. Whenever you see a crack starting to form, take hold of the head and give the whole plant a half turn. What this does is break off some of the roots, which slows the growth of the plant and gives it time to catch up with itself. Give the plant another half turn in a week or so if the cracking continues.

All members of the cabbage family are very shallow-rooted plants. When you transplant them, be sure that you dig a hole deep enough to give the roots a chance to grow down. I know this sounds ridiculous, but if you don't give them a good, deep hole, the roots will actually grow back up toward the surface. Because most of the roots are no more than an inch below the surface, you should be very careful when you cultivate around these plants.

Cabbages, unfortunately, attract quite a few bugs. The cabbage maggot gets into the roots of the plant. This insect can be discouraged with tobacco dust. The green cabbage worm is the larva of the yellow and white butterflies you may have seen flying around your garden. Cabbage worms will eat tremendous holes in the leaves and will ruin the heads if they are allowed to burrow into them. Once again, Bt should take care of them.

You can also try using salt on your cabbages. Take a salt shaker, go out in the morning when the dew is still on the plants, and sprinkle each one. In fact, early morning is the time of the day when you should be doing all of your dusting. The dew will help the dust stick to the plants.

Growing very large heads is a challenge, but I have to admit that I prefer eating the smaller ones. Besides, my family and I can't possibly eat one of those large heads all at one time. We have to cut it in half and save the second part for later in the week. I am sure we get more nourishment when we eat all of a small head at one sitting. To grow smaller heads, I sometimes squeeze the plants a little closer together in the row, planting them 10 inches apart instead of 18. This way, I can grow three heads where I would normally grow two. I use a little more fertilizer this way, but the heads are not so apt to crack.

Carrots

Carrots are like any other root crop. They will do best in loose, sandy soil. But that doesn't mean you can't grow them if the soil in your garden is not sandy. You can make almost any soil loose by tilling it often and by working humus, compost, or leaf mold into it.

You should plant carrots very early in the spring. The seeds are very fine, so it is hard to keep from planting them too thickly. One trick is to mix fine soil with the seed. Carrot seed is slow to germinate, so you might mix in a few fast-sprouting radish seeds to mark the rows.

It is very important to thin carrots. If you don't, you won't get many that are large enough to eat. I thin them first the same way I thin beets, by drawing a steel rake across the row. The rake's teeth will do all the thinning that is necessary. This procedure can be a little frightening at first. In fact, you may think that you have ruined your whole crop. Don't worry; most of the plants will recover and look fine in a day or two. Thinning is always a painful process, but it helps to produce healthier crops in the long run.

Carrots like fertilizer, so give them an ample supply of compost or some commercial fertilizer. Chemical fertilizer can burn tiny carrot seeds, so don't get it too close to them. Be careful about planting carrot seeds too deep. Remember the formula: four times the diameter of the seed.

I find that Half Longs are the best variety for most people. Regular carrots that grow very long and thin have to be grown in sandy loam. If you want tender, young roots all summer long, plant carrots once every three weeks, right into August. The reason for planting late in the season is to have carrots coming to maturity just in time to store them in a root cellar in the fall. An early-August planting will be ready right around the first of October.

The largest carrots, as I already mentioned, are beneath the darkest, greenest tops. This is one way you can tell if a carrot is large enough without pulling it up. Finger-sized carrots are delicious. Don't try to grow the monstrous, prize-winning ones. They are much too tough. Carrots are prime when they have about the same diameter as a quarter. Let them get much bigger and they become "woody"—fibrous and pulpy.

Carrots are almost trouble-free as far as insects are concerned. Plant them, cultivate them once in a while, harvest them, and enjoy them.

Cauliflower

Cauliflower seems to suffer in very hot weather. It should be grown either early in the gardening season or in the fall. In other words, you

should try to avoid having the heads come to maturity in midsummer.

Don't be afraid to start cauliflower indoors quite early. If you harden off the plants properly, there is little chance that they will be killed or injured by an unexpected cold snap. Transplant them a week or two before the last spring frost date, spaced 16 inches apart in a 2–1–2 pattern. When you set them out, firm the soil very tightly around the roots. The idea is to keep excessive air from getting to the root hairs and drying them out.

As cauliflower heads start to form, they should be "blanched." This simply means that you prevent sunlight from reaching the head for a while. Normal blanching time is four to eight days, but it may take a little longer in the fall. Blanching will make the cauliflower white and tender. To do this, pull the large outer leaves up over the top of the head, and tie them there with twine or fasten them with a rubber band. Or you can take a leaf, break it partially, lay it over the top of the cauliflower, and tuck it in on the other side of the head. Break leaves on all four sides, and fold each one over the top. This will let air in but keep sunlight out. I like this method better than tying the leaves together.

Late cauliflower can be started from seed outdoors in early summer. When seedlings are 2 to 3 inches tall, they should be transplanted in rows 2 to 3 feet apart, with 2 feet between each plant. Cauliflower will do poorly in soil that is acidic. It will be quite happy if the pH is right around 7. Acidity encourages a disease in cauliflower called "whip tail."

Celery

Celery seems to require reasonably good, loamy soil. If yours is heavy clay or extremely sandy, it would be best to add organic matter in the form of leaf mold, compost, or manure; otherwise, you are not likely to have good luck with this vegetable. Celery likes fertilizer, so be sure that you keep it well fed.

I start seeds inside three months before the last spring frost date. The seeds are very fine, so you must take care not to plant them too deep. Just sprinkle them in the flat and firm the soil with a board. When the celery plants are 2 inches high, I transplant them. When I transplant most things, either inside or outside, I remove some of the leaves. By doing this, I am intentionally throwing the plant out of balance: I am making the roots stronger in relation to the top of the plant. Eliminating all the extra foliage makes the plant less apt to wilt, and it will eventually grow stronger. When I transplant celery, I pinch off all but the center sprays. Some time after it has been transplanted the first time, I begin to harden celery off. It can be transplanted into my garden a week before the last spring frost date if I have been conscientious about getting the young plants accustomed to the outdoors. If a plant is tall and strong, I put a rubber band around its top to pull it all together for transplanting.

I dig a trench or a furrow—the furrowing attachment on the back of the rotary tiller works just about perfectly—and plant the celery in the bottom. As the plants continue to grow, I keep pulling soil up around them. This is called "hilling." The only part of the plant that shows above the dirt is the topmost tuft of leaves. Keeping the main part of the plant growing below ground level will blanch the stalks.

For a late crop of celery, you can plant seed outside with your other early crops. Celery plants should be spaced no closer than a foot apart after the final transplanting. The spacing between rows is not all that critical.

If hilling celery seems like too much of a job, you can use boards to blanch it. When the plants get to be about 10 inches high, prop a 1" x 10" board up against either side of the row. Fasten the tops of the planks together with a small wooden cleat or with wire so they won't blow over on a windy day. After two or three weeks of being shaded like this, the plants should be white and succulent.

Try self-blanching varieties of celery if you want, but the easiest thing is not to blanch celery at all. I think that green celery is a real delicacy. You may find, though, that the crop you grow at home tastes a little stronger than the celery you buy at the store.

Celery will appreciate lots of cultivation, but its roots are near the surface. Don't scratch too deeply with your cultivating tool or you may damage the plants.

Celery and warm weather do not mix well. Plan to have an early crop and a late crop, and avoid trying to produce good stalks during the hottest summer months. If you begin blanching in early fall, using the hilling technique, you will be insulating the stalks against cold at the same time. The crop should last until long after frost has set in. In fact, you can store celery right in the ground until well into winter if you put a good thick mulch over it.

Not many insects are attracted to celery, so there is no need to use insecticides. You can start harvesting as soon as the stalks are as big around as a pencil. These are delicious. Larger, outside stalks which come along later can be used in soups or as a garnish.

Celeriac

Celeriac can be grown like celery, except that it does not have to be blanched. Its thick roots are delicious in soups, in salads, or just by themselves. The seed can be sown very early, so there is no reason to start plants inside. Plant the seeds about an inch apart. When the plants are 3 inches high, more or less, transplant them into rows 12 to 18 inches apart. Leave 6 inches between plants.

If you're going to transplant celeriac, soak the ground with water beforehand. It seems to enjoy muddiness—for a while at least. Try to keep as much of the original soil as possible around the roots when you move the plant. Dig in under the roots with your hand and squeeze the plant with your fingers to keep the soil in contact with the roots. If you expose them to too much oxygen during transplanting, they will dry out very quickly and the plant will die.

I recommend the Snowball variety of celeraic. This has round, smooth roots about 3 inches across.

Chicory

Chicory is a green that grows wild in most sections of the country. You can recognize it by its little blue flowers. You have probably seen it growing in fields and along the roadside. It is a very tough plant, mainly because its deep root system permits it to grow in any kind of soil, even very dry hardpan. The young tops can be eaten very much the same way that you eat endive.

Chicory can be planted in the late spring or early summer. The plants should be at least 6 inches apart in rows spaced at least 2 feet apart. They will grow to be 2 to 4 feet high without much further assistance from you. Cut the tops off within an inch or two of the crown when you want greens.

The roots can be harvested after there has been a killing frost. Cut back whatever tops remain, and trim off some of the root—which by this time will be very long. Store these roots in a box of sand or fresh sawdust. In the middle of winter, you can "force" them simply by starting to water them. In about three weeks, they will start to send out tender, white shoots, which are a very tasty salad item. A good time to dig wild chicory is in the fall. Force them if you like, or store them and plant them in your garden in the spring.

Chinese Cabbage

Chinese cabbage has a long and compact head. When you take off the outer leaves, it looks a little like a tight bunch of celery. The light green leaves have a crisp, nutty flavor. I understand that the Chinese use this vegetable in practically all their cooking, but our family uses it mainly for salads.

Chinese cabbage does best in cool weather. It can be started indoors, but should stay in seed flats no longer than about four weeks before it is transplanted outside. Most of the outer leaves should be stripped off when you transplant. The cabbages should be set out approximately 12 inches apart with 2 feet of space between rows.

In the North, your fall crop can be planted the last week of July or the first week of August. Plant the seeds right where you want the plants to be so you won't have to transplant. They will grow very rapidly, because there will be no transplanting shock to set them back. Your late crop may turn out better than your first. Bugs and worms do not seem to bother them as much in the fall as they do during the summer. In fact, my suggestion to someone trying Chinese cabbage for the first time would be to plant only a fall crop directly from seed. As transplants, they can be planted in a 3–2–3 pattern in a 20-inch wide row. A spring crop requires a lot more care and attention. If you don't look after the plants and dust them almost daily, the outer leaves will soon be riddled with insect holes. This looks unattractive, but the inner leaves usually remain untouched and suitable for harvest.

Chives

Every garden should have some chives. They are a perennial, so once you plant them you can have them year after year. Chives, as you probably know, are a member of the onion family. It would be impossible to list all the good uses that chives can be put to. They add a zesty flavor to almost any dish.

Plant chives where they can stay undisturbed for several years. You can start them inside, but wait until the soil warms up in the spring before transplanting them outside. They are attractive enough to be planted in borders along with flowers. One or 2 square feet devoted to chives should meet your needs.

Chives are almost completely disease-free. After they have been growing for a couple of years, you can separate the plant clusters and expand your bed by moving some of the plants elsewhere. In the fall, you can take up part of a cluster, plant it in a pot indoors, and have fresh chives all winter. Clip off the tops whenever you need them. It is almost impossible, I think, to cut them so much that they can't recover and grow more. And, best of all, chives will put out lovely pinkish blossoms sometime in the middle of the summer.

Collards

Collards are members of the cabbage family. They like the same soil as cabbages, and they are susceptible to cabbage diseases and may be attacked by the same insects. They too need to be treated regularly with Bt to control insect damage.

Collards can stand hot weather as well as or better than any other vegetable in the garden. This is one reason why they do very well in the South. They can be grown directly from seed. Plant collards in a 16-inch wide row and thin the young plants to a 2–1–2 pattern with plants spaced 16 inches apart. They form no heads; we are interested in the leaves themselves. These can be blanched either by tying the leaves together or by putting a rubber band around them. Blanching is, of course, not necessary.

No member of the cabbage family should be planted in the same spot two years in a row. This rule applies to collards.

Corn

Sweet corn will grow in almost any kind of soil, but it will do best in light, sandy loam. The reason for this is simple if you think about it. Sandy soil dries out quickly in the spring. It also tends to warm up faster than heavy clay. You can usually plant corn many days—even weeks—earlier in lighter soil.

Here in Vermont, I have sweet corn as early as two weeks before anyone else, even before the commercial growers. My method is quite simple—although I should admit that it took me nearly ten years to figure it out.

I try to have corn planted by my birthday, April 13, which is very early for Vermont. Most people here don't plan on planting corn

PLANTING IN FURROWS

I like to plant sweet corn in furrows. I use the furrower behind my rototiller, which makes a furrow about 4 or 5 inches deep. I plant my corn in the bottom of these furrows, covering it with the usual amount of soil. Do not fill the furrow to the top. Because we have bird problems, I purchased some 12-inch-wide chicken wire with 1½-inch mesh. I lay this right over the top of each furrow so the birds cannot get at the corn until it is well established. Once the corn gets up to the chicken wire, I roll it up and take it off the field.

Planting in deep furrows has another advantage. When it rains, water will collect in these furrows. The extra moisture encourages the corn to germinate very fast. Once you start to cultivate with the tiller, dirt tumbles down into the furrow in which you planted and your corn is automatically hilled. The dirt also covers up a good share of the weeds and saves you a lot of weeding. After a couple of cultivations, the furrow will be filled up level, and your corn will stand up much better in the wind.

Another way to keep the birds from getting your corn is to run two strings parallel, about 2 inches apart, and 4 inches above the row. (Fishing line works well.) When a bird reaches in to pull out a kernel of corn, the back of his head bumps these strings. This usually scares him so badly that he forgets all about the corn. You can also make a long "pyramid" of chicken wire down the length of each row. Just unroll your chicken wire and bend it in half lengthwise. This works very well. Of course, chicken wire lasts for many, many years, so it is well worth the initial investment.

much before May 15 or 20. Choose a place where there is no sod, little fresh organic matter in the soil, and no cover crop. (Annual ryegrass might be all right in this spot, because it will be dead and gone by the time spring arrives.)

If you have an area in your garden that slopes slightly to the south or west, great! This is the perfect spot for early crops, because the soil will be much warmer there. Till this area as soon as you can work the soil, but put nothing on it—*no manures, no fertilizers*. Plant your corn in rows, but plant it a trifle deeper than you would ordinarily—slightly more than four times the diameter of the seed. Normal planting depth for corn is about 1 inch. Plant early corn about 1½ inches deep.

Remember: *use absolutely no fertilizer or organic matter*. If you do, the seed may rot! Be patient. It may take six weeks or so for your corn to come up. Eventually, it will sprout and put out a root system, but it might just hover there until the temperature gets right. Then it will suddenly put in an appearance. I have found that it can stand two or three frosts once it has come up. I have seen my early sweet corn lying frozen right on the ground and completely brown. To my surprise, it came right back up. If you put fertilizer near the seed, though, the seedling will grow so fast and so tender that a good freeze or frost will kill it for sure. Organic matter or manure in the soil will encourage microorganisms to start working there. This will cause the early corn to have very, very tender roots. The microbes may even start to decompose the roots themselves. Obviously, it makes sense

to plant an early variety if you want early corn. Span Cross, Butter and Sugar, and Sugar and Gold work very well. I have also had good luck with early plantings of some midseason varieties.

Corn likes two things—hot weather and lots of fertilizer. It should be, as the old farmers say, "knee high by the Fourth of July." You can plant corn either in hills or in rows. If you choose the hill method, you should plant four or five seeds in each hill. When the plants come up, thin to four seedlings per hill.

I like to plant my corn in rows rather than in hills. I find that if you plant a seed once every 8 to 10 inches in a straight row, the plants are better nourished. Hills force the root systems of the plants to compete with each other for nutrients and moisture. By the time corn is knee-high, its roots will extend about 15 inches in all directions. Plant three or four short rows of each variety, rather than one long row, for better pollination.

Don't forget that corn requires a large investment of garden space for a relatively small return, and it ties up the space for a long time. One of the advantages of growing early corn is that, after harvesting it, you still have time to plant and harvest a crop of beets, lettuce, chard, or late beans. Corn, as you know, is very tall when it reaches its full growth. Plant it on the north or east side of your garden so that it will not shade your other crops.

Try to plant more than one variety of corn if you have the space—an early, a midseason, and a late variety. Late corn tastes the best. Silver Queen is one of the best varieties of late corn I know of, but unfortunately it has a 90-

day growing time. Here in Vermont, it doesn't mature until September, but it is well worth waiting for.

Cultivation is essential, but keep in mind that the roots of cornstalks grow fairly close to the surface of the ground. Don't go deeper than an inch or an inch and a half at the most. Keep the weeds down in your cornfield. It is too easy to neglect them. Because corn grows high, it sometimes seems hard to believe that weeds can get the upper hand. Don't let them compete with the corn for fertilizer and moisture; they will steal a lot of it, and corn needs all the nutrients it can get!

I do not recommend that you pick the suckers off the sides of cornstalks as some people do. Some varieties put out several suckers, each of which will bear an ear of corn if the plants are well side-dressed with fertilizer. Corn should first be side-dressed when it is 8 or 10 inches high. You can side-dress a second time when the corn silks first appear. The second side-dressing will encourage the plant to produce full ears.

Earworms are a problem to corn growers everywhere in the country. The earworm works his way through the outer husk and feeds on the kernels inside. If you find one, or evidence of one, in an ear of corn, you don't have

FREEZING CORN

Mr. and Mrs. James E. Speight of Whites Creek, Tennessee, use a large-eared, white variety of corn called Silver Mine for freezing. This variety is used only for cutting off the cob. A smaller, yellow corn like Golden Bantam is used for freezing on the cob.

Here is the Speights' recipe for freezing corn:

Cut the corn off and scrape all the milk from the cob. Then prepare the corn as if you're fixing it for the table. Season it with a little sugar, salt, and flour, add a little vegetable oil, then cook just until the mixture starts to thicken. Take it from the stove, allow it to cool thoroughly, bag it, and place in the freezer. When preparing the corn to eat, add some butter and cook for a short time in a skillet.

When the Speights take this to a covered-dish social at the church, everybody wants to know the secret of freezing such great-tasting corn.

to throw the whole thing away. Cut out the bad part and enjoy the rest. Dusting with rotenone discourages earworms. So does a drop of mineral oil placed in the corn silk just as it begins to form. You may also have an invasion of European corn borers from time to time. I am sorry to admit that I know of no spray that discourages them.

It is nice to be able to pick fresh corn over a long period of time. This is the best reason for planting both early and late varieties. A packet of seeds will tell you how long the corn inside will take to mature. Early varieties are usually ready about 10 weeks after sowing; later ones normally need about 10 to 12 weeks.

Harvest corn when the kernels are at the "milky" stage. Make a little slit in the husk while it is still on the stalk. If the kernels look full and yellow, give one of them the thumbnail test. If white liquid squirts out, the corn is of excellent quality and is ready to eat.

Whether you are going to eat it fresh, can it, or freeze it, you should have everything ready to cook or process corn immediately. The old maxim that says you should "have the water boiling before you pick the corn" is true. As soon as the ears are off the stalk, the sugars in the kernels begin turning to starch, and the flavor begins to decline. There is nothing like fresh corn picked from the garden just before supper.

As soon as your corn crop is harvested, dispose of the residue. Don't leave the stalks standing in the field or you will encourage disease, earworms, and borers in future crops. The best way to dispose of cornstalks is to till them into the soil. This provides good nourishment for your friends, the earthworms and microorganisms. If you don't have any way to till your corn wastes under efficiently, compost them, either in an active compost pile or by throwing them in a trench and covering with 3 or 4 inches of soil. Don't burn or throw away cornstalks. Use them to build up the humus content of your soil.

Corn that you plan to freeze should mature in September or later, when it will be at its sweetest. There is not much point in freezing corn that ripens in July. By the time you eat it in the winter, it will have been in the freezer too long to taste really good.

Cucumbers

Cucumbers are a very tender crop. Normally, you should not plant them without some sort of protection until all danger of frost has passed. This means late May where I live, but I have a plan that lets me get started a little earlier than this. I sprout cucumber seeds in wet paper towels, plant the seedlings under hotcaps about two weeks before the average date of the last killing frost, and leave the hotcaps on until I am pretty sure there will be no more freezing temperatures. This is one way to get cukes before most other people do.

You can also start them inside, but not until about three or four weeks before you are going

to set them out. If you start them too early, they will get too big too fast. It is a good idea to plant seeds either in a cube of sod (see instructions on page 41), or in peat or "jiffy" pots. These containers can be transplanted right into the garden soil without disturbing the tender cucumber roots.

Under normal conditions, cucumber seeds can be planted in hills, in mounds, or in rows about ten days after the last frost date. I can hear you asking, "What is the difference between a hill and a mound?" A hill is an area a few inches in diameter where you plant six, eight, or ten seeds in a circle. A mound is a place where you have built up the soil, added manure, and planted seeds on top of the hump. If your soil is wet and heavy, a mound would be more advantageous than just a hill. A mound gives your plants drier feet. Heavy soil will grow larger cucumbers than sandy soil, by the way.

I have light soil, so I like to plant cucumbers in rows. If you grow them in hills, your plants tend to be concentrated in one area. As soon as the seedlings come up, tiny black flies and other insects may invade them. They may eat the tender leaves of the plants as soon as they appear above ground. These bugs congregate for food, yes, but they are also there to mate. If one stops by your cucumber patch, another will stop, and before you know it, you have a whole troop of them. If you happen to be away for a day or two, or if you don't catch them in time, they will devour the whole hill. If your cucumbers are planted in a row and the bugs attack, they might destroy a chunk of the row, but they probably won't wipe out the entire planting. The surviving plants will fill in that area again.

I plant cucumber seeds 6 to 8 inches apart in the row. First I put in some good compost or manure, cover it with about 2 inches of soil, then plant the seeds. I usually plant radishes among them. Radishes help a lot, because that troublesome little black fly will eat the radish leaves before he gets interested in the cucumber plants.

If you use the mound or the hill method, build your mounds every 4 feet in rows about 6 feet apart so that you will have room later to walk between the rows. If you plant eight or ten seeds in a hill, let them grow four or five leaves apiece; then pull up the weaker plants, leaving only five. These five seedlings will then have plenty of room to grow.

Cucumbers seem to consume lots of fertilizer. If you do nothing else to prepare your soil, you should at least mix in an ample amount of fertilizer before you plant. If you use a chemical fertilizer, don't do this immediately before you sow or the fertilizer will burn the seed. Give yourself a couple of days' leeway between fertilizing and planting to allow the chemicals to dissolve in the soil.

A side-dressing is great for cucumbers. The best time to do this is just before the vines have started to crawl along the ground. The plant will stand up and grow about a foot tall before it lies down and starts to spread out in all directions. Hoe a very shallow trench on either side of your rows or in a circle around the mounds or hills. Don't make this indentation any closer than 4 inches from the centers of the plants.

Sprinkle compost, organic fertilizer, manure, or a commercial fertilizer like 10–10–10 in the trench, and cover it with soil. If the leaves or stems make contact with the fertilizer, they will be burned. The fertilizer should take effect just as the plants blossom—the time when they need nutrients the most if they are going to produce an abundant crop.

Plant two or three varieties of cukes. Some will do better in a given year than others, depending on the weather. I always plant picklers because they bear very early. If you are smart enough to plant dill just as soon as the ground can be worked in the spring, your dill should be ready about the time the early cukes are ready for pickling. I think a lot of people are afraid to pick little cucumbers because they are afraid they won't get any more. Actually, if you keep picking the baby cucumbers, the plant will never get a chance to produce good, big seeds, and it will continue to blossom and bear. Harvest all the small cucumbers you want during the summer, and I can assure you that you will have bushels more by fall.

You should try to control the growth of cucumber vines. When they have grown about 3 feet to either side of the row, I like to stop them. I am not looking for record-breaking vines, after all; I am looking for lots of good vegetables. You will find a little fuzzy tuft at the end of each vine. It looks like a cottontail, and is about the size of your little finger. If you pinch this off with your fingers, the vine won't grow any farther. Every time I pick cucumbers, I also pinch off a bunch of these little fuzzy ends. Of course, the plant may send out a new vine once you do this; wait until another fuzzy end appears and pick it off. This does less damage to the plant than actually cutting the vines themselves.

You can do the same thing with squash and pumpkins. Picking off the fuzzy ends allows the plant to put more strength into the vegetables. If you grow cucumbers on a trellis or on a fence, stop their growth when they reach the top. There is no point in letting them grow back down the other side.

Dill

Dill is used primarily in making pickles, but it can also add a little extra flavor to much of your cooking and salad-making. Plant dill very early in the spring so that the heads will ripen just as your cucumber plants start to produce their first small cucumbers. This is the time when you should be making your first batches of pickles. Dill can be planted in a wide row or small block. It usually re-seeds itself if left to mature and will give you a small crop of foliage in the same year and full plants the following year.

It may take one to two weeks for dill seed to come up. It is another of the crops that should be marked with radish seeds. I like to plant dill in wide rows. Three feet of 10-inch-wide row gives me all I need for pickles, salads, sauces, and seeds for next year's crop. Dill can also be grown successfully in a pot inside the house.

The feathery dill leaves can be harvested anytime. If you want to save the seed heads, cut them just before they turn dark brown. If you wait much longer, the seeds will start falling off. Hang the heads up to dry, and you can use them throughout the winter. Fresh-cut heads, harvested just before they are ripe, have the most dill flavor. These are ideal for use in pickling if you've timed your cucumber harvest right.

Eggplant

Eggplant will do fine in a well-drained, sandy soil, but it is extremely tender and can't stand frost. In fact, it likes heat almost as much as it likes fertilizer.

Eggplants should be planted in 2-foot wide rows in a 3–2–3 pattern, in rows spaced about 2 feet apart. It is best to use plants that are anywhere from four to eight weeks old. Wrap a piece of newspaper around each plant for cutworm protection. Eggplants need to be watched very closely. Bugs, especially aphids and potato bugs, like them, so they will either have to be sprayed from time to time or the bugs will have to be picked off by hand. Look under the leaves for egg cases and crush them. Cultivate gently and not too deeply around eggplants; their roots are very close to the surface, as are the roots of most other heat-loving plants. They are finicky about moisture and will suffer if their water supply is not regular.

You can start to eat eggplant as soon as they appear shiny, and you can continue to eat them long after they have matured. There is no need to pick them as soon as they ripen.

Endive

Endive can be treated and cared for very much like lettuce. You can plant it in either wide or single rows. Harvest it just the way you would harvest leaf lettuce—by cutting down the whole plant.

Endive can be planted very early because it is quite frost-resistant. I find that in warmer weather it has a tendency to become bitter. The best times to sow endive seed are around the first of May and then again around the first of August. I think that fall endive is better than the early crop, but this may have something to do with our cool Vermont autumns.

You can blanch endive and reduce its bitterness by gathering up the leaves and putting a rubber band around the top of the plant. It takes two to three weeks to blanch it properly. Moisture can gather in the inner leaves and cause rotting during this time, so it is important to harvest the plant as soon as the blanching is finished.

Garlic

Garlic is a member of the onion family, but, instead of producing one bulb, it produces a group of small bulbs called *cloves*. The cultural recommendations for garlic are very similar to those for onions. You should plant them in the spring. Break the bulb up into individual cloves. You may get as many as 15 from a single bulb. You can plant them in a row, but I prefer to plant them in a wide row so they will take up less room in the garden. Garlic likes fertilizer, so add either a complete fertilizer or some organic fertilizer—compost, manure, blood meal, or bonemeal.

When the tops fall over or die in the fall, pull up the bulbs and let them dry in the sun for a few days, just as you would do with onions. Then put them in a mesh bag and hang it in an airy place for a week or two before storing the bulbs in the cellar.

Planting garlic in the spring produces an average garlic bulb, but if you want to get large garlic, plant the cloves in the fall. Set fall-planted garlic about 3 inches deep; spring garlic should be planted very shallow.

Garlic is widely used for flavoring foods, but it is also used to make a brew to spray on plants to repel insects. Organic gardeners use this simple brew successfully on a lot of different plants, but you do have to spray on a daily basis.

Horseradish

I love horseradish. People are amazed to see so much of it growing in my garden. What they don't understand is that I eat horseradish each and every morning with eggs! This breakfast diet probably won't appeal to you as much as it does to me, so you probably won't want to grow quite as much as I do.

Horseradish is one of the easiest crops to raise because it spreads so rapidly. The simplest way to get started is to send away by mail for some root cuttings. The root cuttings will arrive with the small end cut on a slant. These should be planted about 2 inches below the surface of the soil with the small end down. Give them a little fertilizer, and they will grow like mad. Before you know it, you will have huge plants.

Horseradish tends to take over, so you should give some thought to the location of your planting. It can spread to other parts of the garden and, once it gets there, it will be hard to get rid of. You only need to buy half a dozen roots. This will give you and several of your neighbors more than enough to eat.

The roots can be dug in the fall like carrots or beets, but you can dig them and use them at any time of year. Store them right in the garden if you like and dig them up in the spring. They will be stronger.

A kitchen blender is a great device for making horseradish sauce; it isn't as tear-jerking a process as grating the roots by hand. Put sliced horseradish roots, water, and a few drops of distilled white vinegar in the blender, and grind the mixture to whatever texture you want. Keep the sauce refrigerated or it will lose its color and flavor. Ground horseradish keeps very well when canned or flash-frozen. Frozen roots are fine for grinding during the off-season.

Jerusalem Artichokes

The nicest thing about Jerusalem artichokes is that they are almost completely free of diseases and pests. Believe it or not, they are related to the sunflower. They are very prolific—so prolific that, if you do not watch them closely, they will try to take over your whole garden.

Jerusalem artichokes are grown for their underground tubers, which are both delicious and low in calories. (They are very good for diabetics, incidentally.) They will grow just about anywhere in the United States. They can be planted either in the fall or in the spring as soon as the ground can be worked. The easiest way to start them is by planting enough tubers for a 25-foot row. Bury them about 2 feet apart. It is best to leave at least 3 feet between rows; 4 feet is even better. When it is mature, a Jerusalem artichoke plant will be 6 or 8 feet tall, so be sure to plant them where they will not shade other plants in the garden.

Jerusalem artichokes need a very long growing season—about 125 days. Harvest them after the frost has killed the tops. They can be dug anytime during the fall and winter months.

There are a number of good ways to eat Jerusalem artichokes. Cook them or eat them raw in salads. I like them boiled. They are also good cut into small pieces and cooked in a cream sauce.

Kale

Kale is one of the garden's freaks. It is probably the hardiest green of all. You can harvest kale from under the snow in the dead of winter. It will grow 12 months of the year.

Kale seems to do even better in cool weather than it does in the heat of summer.

And I think it tastes best after the weather has been cold for a while. You might plant some early, some in midseason, and some late. It will do well in almost any kind of soil, but it should be well fertilized.

Rows of kale should be set 2 feet apart, and the plants should have anywhere from 6 inches to a foot of space between them. Kale does well in wide rows. The same insects that like cabbage also like kale. This is another reason why the crop that comes along in September, October, or November is the best one; there are fewer bugs around to infest it.

Too many people pull up or till under kale plants in the fall. I get upset when I see this. Let your kale keep growing right into winter. Fresh kale greens will be a real delicacy in February when you are beginning to get tired of canned and frozen vegetables. The deeper the snow, the better it tastes!

You can cook kale the same way you cook spinach; you can use it in soups and for stir-frying; you can eat it raw in salads; or you can use it as a garnish for other dishes. Two good varieties are Blue Curled Scotch and Siberian. I think I prefer the former.

Kohlrabi

Kohlrabi is another member of the cabbage family. You eat the large base of the stem, which looks something like a turnip that has formed above ground. The best ones are those that have grown quickly; those that grow slowly are usually tough and woody. A side-dressing of fertilizer will help to speed up growth.

Try to use kohlrabi before it has had a chance to mature completely. It should be ready 10 to 12 weeks after the seeds are planted. The seeds are hardy, which means that they can be sown early—either outside in the garden or in a cold frame. The plants should be 5 to 6 inches apart in rows. Kohlrabi does well in wide-row plantings. Cultivate them regularly. Once the bottom of the stem has reached 2 to 3 inches in diameter, it is ready to eat.

Lettuce

No one ever argues with me when I say that lettuce is the world's most popular salad plant. One of the reasons for this may be that it grows well almost anywhere.

If you have ever pulled up a lettuce plant of any kind, I am sure you were surprised to see how small and shallow the root system was. This explains why lettuce needs well-fertilized soil. The roots do not go deep enough to bring up nutrients that have drained out of the upper layers of soil.

Plant lettuce when you plant peas, as soon as the ground can be worked in the spring. It will do well in late March, April, and May, and it can stand a number of freezes. It does not do very well in the heat of summer, but you can sow it again in late July, early August, or September and have an excellent late crop.

I am convinced that planting lettuce seed in wide rows is the best method, but it will do well in single rows, too. If you do choose a wide row, you will discover that you need only about 3 to 5 feet of any one variety. This should leave you room to experiment with several varieties at once. In a single row, you will need about 20 feet of each variety to have enough for a family of four.

There are four basic types of lettuce.

1. *Head* (or *Iceberg*) *lettuce* is the kind you probably see most often in your local grocery store. (It may be the only kind you see there.) Great Lakes, Ithaca, Imperial, and Pennlake are all good head-lettuce varieties.

2. The leaves of *Butterhead lettuce* are more loosely folded than head-lettuce leaves. Some good Butterhead varieties are Bibb, Buttercrunch, Deertongue, Big Boston, and Dark Green Boston.

3. There are many different kinds of *Leaf lettuce*; all have comparatively loose, open growth habits. Salad Bowl, Black-Seeded Simpson, and Grand Rapids all produce dense clumps of crinkled, light green leaves. The leaves of Oakleaf, Prizehead, and Ruby range from bronze to red in color.

4. *Cos* or *Romaine lettuce* grows 8 to 9 inches tall; its upright leaves are tightly folded. Dark Green Cos and Parris Island Cos are two widely popular varieties.

Here in Vermont, tight-head lettuce almost has to be started inside and later transplanted outside if it is to be a success. The plants can be set out when they are about 3 inches tall. They should be spaced about 18 inches apart if you are interested in growing large heads. I personally prefer smaller heads, so I plant them 8 to 10 inches apart in wide rows in a 3–2–3 pattern. This way I get more heads, and most are just the right size to eat at one sitting.

When transplanting, all of the outer leaves should be stripped off the plant. After all, it is the center of the plant, the head, that we want to grow. All plants grow from the center out and up. Removing the outer leaves makes the top of the plant smaller in comparison to the root structure. This way, the roots will have time to gain the strength they need to produce strong tops later on.

Lots of people who plant head lettuce think they must wait until it heads up before eating it. Actually, the leaves of all varieties of head lettuce can be eaten long before the head appears. This is not a bad idea. As long as you keep it cut, it will never form a head. Loose-head lettuce leaves are tastier and crunchier than some leaf varieties.

There are some diseases, blights, and insects that bother lettuce, but they do not seem to show up too often. You should not have to worry about dusting and spraying. Once in a while, a cutworm will get into your lettuce and do a little harm, but cutworms will rarely damage your whole crop. Trying to keep them out is hardly worth the effort.

Make several succession plantings of lettuce, using a number of different varieties. If you do, you should have fresh lettuce from May to October. Late in the fall, after frost has really set in, you can take up a few plants from the garden, put them in flats, and bring them inside to continue growing throughout the winter in a sunny window. And you can grow lettuce in an outdoor cold frame for a very early spring harvest. It is entirely possible to grow fresh lettuce year-round; you may never have to buy it from a grocery store again.

Remember when you harvest lettuce that you want to cut the leaves a little above the ground, not pull them up. A second crop will grow where you cut the plants.

Melons

Because of the climate here in Vermont, we are severely limited when it comes to growing decent melons. There is no way to get ahead of Mother Nature. But there are a few things you can do to gain a week or so.

The ideal soil for muskmelons is well-drained, sandy loam in a sunny spot. In northern states, it helps to have a garden spot that slopes slightly to the south or the southeast. Generally, melons like a lot of sun, dry feet, and lots of fertilizer. They do best when planted in hills with four plants to each hill. If you have compost, put some under each hill. If you have no compost or manure, mix a little extra fertilizer into the soil. I like to plant a few radishes around each hill to give the insects something to munch on besides the tiny melon leaves.

About a week before the last spring frost, I take four paper towels from a roll, wet them, and fold them back on each other so that they are the size of one. I sprinkle my melon seeds on this wet towel and roll it up like a cinnamon twirl. Then I soak a terrycloth face towel with all the water it will hold. I wrap the rolled paper towels inside this and put the whole thing inside a plastic bag. Then I put the plastic bag in a spot where the temperature stays around 70°F. (21°C.).

In four or five days, the seeds will have sprouted. I prepare the melon hills and buy some hotcaps, the waxed-paper kind, to protect the young plants from frost. I take the wet towels out into the garden and very carefully unwrap them. I usually find that most of the seeds have sprouted. Those few that haven't probably would not have germinated in the soil, either. I plant these sprouts just as though I were planting seeds. If I want five plants to a hill, I plant six or seven seeds, just in case one or two don't make it. I make a hole with my finger, drop a sprout into it, and cover it with enough soil to equal four times the diameter of the seed. Then I cover it with a hotcap.

I don't have to worry about the melons again until the first of June. The hotcaps will protect the tiny plants from frost and insects and will hold the heat in the soil beneath them. Hotcaps can help you gain a week or more with your melons.

Melon seeds tend to be poor germinators. If they are planted without sprouting first, and then are not warmed and protected by hotcaps, only one or two seeds might come up in each hill. I use this sprouting technique with many different crops that I think need a head start. I have made it work with cucumbers, beans, onions, corn, beets, and squash. Years ago, when I sold vegetables from a stand in front of my house, I could get a week's jump on some of my competition by sprouting seeds this way. Sprouting eliminates guesswork. Wherever you plant a sprouted seed, you can be sure a plant will grow.

Melons are heat-loving plants, so, while the young plants are growing, I try to remember to save tin cans of all kinds. After the vines start to bear and the melons get a little bigger than a baseball, I use the cans to hold the fruit up off the ground. To do so, I carefully lift each small melon, then I push an upside-down can into the soil underneath it so that only 2 or 3 inches of the can shows above ground. Then I place the melon on top of the can. Sometimes I punch a hole in the top of the can so that rainwater will run out of it. Melons, as I said, like heat, but they don't normally get enough

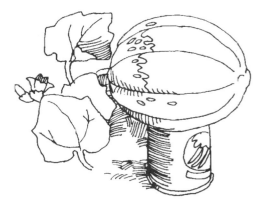

To get ripe melons a week early, carefully place young fruits on upside-down tin cans. The cans will keep these melons warmer than those sitting on the cool ground.

GOOD TASTIN' CANTALOUPES

One happy gardener, Fred Tucker, takes great pride in growing the largest, best-tasting cantaloupes in the town of Big Pool, Maryland. Here's how he does it:

"Around the middle of April I spread a 20' x 50' area with old horse manure that doesn't contain much straw. Then I rototill this in. At this time, I plant Heart of Gold seed in peat pots. These begin growing in my cold frame, or you could use a windowsill.

"In three to four weeks, I rototill the plot again, adding another bushel or two of horse manure. Then I wait until at least June to set my plants out. There is a saying here in Maryland, 'Plant cantaloupes in May—you'll throw them away. Plant them in June, and they'll come just as soon.'

"Cantaloupes love water, so if I don't get rain, I water often. I rototill again before the plants send out long runners. That's my method, and I have plenty to eat and give away many, many more."

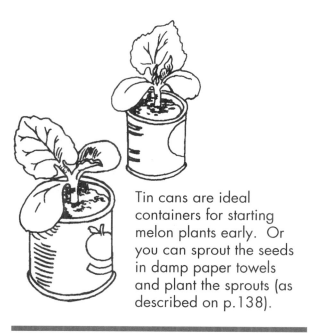

Tin cans are ideal containers for starting melon plants early. Or you can sprout the seeds in damp paper towels and plant the sprouts (as described on p.138).

here in Vermont when they lie directly on the cool ground. The bottom of a melon placed on a can is warmed, so it will ripen at least a week earlier than those grown the normal way. Melons grown on tin cans are much sweeter than others because they are much riper. I have also seen some people use aluminum pie plates for this purpose; I have tried this variation myself, but I think the cans work better.

The same bugs that like cucumbers also like muskmelons, but they can be discouraged by dusting with rotenone. Watch out for cutworms. A newspaper collar will protect transplants against them.

About the first week of August, I pick off the ends of all my melon vines. The melons are still growing or are just starting to ripen at this point. During the last week of August, I pick off the smaller green melons, leaving only the ones that I think will ripen before frost. This allows all of the plant's strength to go into the fruit left on the vine. I keep controlling the growth of the melon plants by continuing to pick off the fuzzy ends of the vines.

How do you know when a melon is ripe? Try smelling it. If you know what a muskmelon smells like and you get a strong muskmelon smell, it is probably ripe. In any case, the stem will break off a ripe melon easily.

Onions

I sometimes tell people that you have to use a hammer if you want to kill an onion. They seem to stand all kinds of abuse. They will grow in practically any kind of soil and, if you fertilize them well, they will give you a tremendous yield.

Most vegetables like humus-rich soil, and onions are no exception. They won't mind it a bit if you add some manure or compost to the plot where they will be planted. If you are going to plant onions in rows, put some of this rich organic matter in the furrows.

There are several ways to plant onions. You can grow them from plants, from "sets" (little onions that grow up to be big onions), or you can grow them directly from seed. Start onions very early, regardless of which method you use. Frost will not hurt them. You can put them in just as soon as the frost is out of the ground and you can walk in the garden.

I like to use the wide-row method with onions. I plant radishes with them, as I do with so many other things. I do the first thinning of onions planted from seed by dragging a rake across the row. (Don't do this with onion sets.) Then I wait for the tops to grow a little bit before I thin again. I pull up some to use as scallions. After the final thinning, the remaining onions should stand about 3 inches apart. Large Bermuda onions are an exception. These should have at least 4 inches of space in all directions.

Onions, if they are going to be good ones, demand lots of cultivation. They are also very intolerant of weeds. If you want to grow very large onions, you will have to move some of the dirt away from the bulb. The onion should look as if it is hardly in the ground at all, with only the bottom third or so underground. This gives the onion lots of room to expand. Moving the dirt away takes lots of careful, patient work on your part, but, like so many other things in the garden, it is worth the effort.

Onions started from sets seem to want to go to seed quite quickly. You will have to see that they don't. A small seedpod, which looks a lot like the dome on a Russian Orthodox church, will start to form on the onion top. (The domes were designed to look like onion seedpods.) This seedpod must be removed; otherwise, the bulb on the bottom will become small and tough. You can snap the pod off very easily with your fingers as soon as it appears.

The nicest time to have onions ripen is in the late fall—just in time for storage. I eat most of the ones that were started early from sets during the summer. Once the tops are dead, you should harvest the onions within a week or ten days. If you leave them in the ground too long after the tops have turned brown, the onions will start to rot. Sometimes they will start to grow entirely new tops. Don't let this happen. Once it does, the onion is ruined for storage.

After you pull up your onions, let them sit in the sun to dry. The point of drying them is to kill the little root system at the bottom of each bulb. Each root should look like a very fine wire and be dry and brittle. When the roots are thoroughly dry, you can easily break them off with a wipe of your hand. Drying may take as long as several weeks.

I usually dig up my onions and put them along the side of the driveway to dry. Then I grade them according to size, put them in onion bags, hang them in the garage, and leave them there for three or four weeks. Later, in November, when the temperature is getting down around 25°F. at night pretty consistently, I move them into the cellar. I find that the more I dry the onions, the better they store.

Most onion sets that you grow yourself keep very well. So will Yellow Globe onions, but I don't have such good luck with the Bermuda and Utah varieties. They will be all right until about February, but they will not last all winter. If you can, hang your onion bags from the ceiling of the root cellar. It is a little warmer there than down near the floor. But don't hang the bags too close together. Leave room for plenty of air circulation. This way, your onions will keep their garden-fresh flavor for months.

It is ridiculous to buy onion sets year after year if you have enough room to grow your own. I try to plant some onion seeds sometime in July. I plant them very thickly, in bands about a foot wide. I fertilize them and let them grow, without ever bothering to thin them. Near the end of September, I break over the tops. I don't pull them then; I wait until the second week in October. Then I pull them up, dry them just the way I would dry larger onions, and let them hang from the ceiling of the root cellar until spring, when they will be planted again.

I have found that I can plant onions from seed in August, or even as late as the first part of September. I plant these in bands, too—

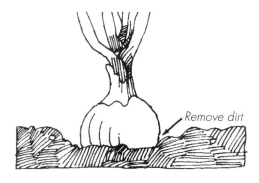

Remove dirt

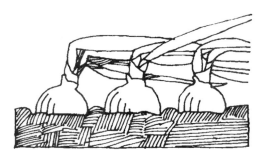

Move dirt away from the bulb so that only one-third is underground. Harvest your onions within a week or ten days of the time the tops fall over and turn brown.

---

sometimes 4 feet wide. I rake the seeds into the ground and leave them there to grow as long as they will. Around the first of November, I break down the tops and mulch the onions with no more than 3 inches of leaves or hay. In the spring, after the snow is gone, I remove the mulch, and in a very short time, I have small onions growing green tops. Some of these can be used as onion plants in another part of the garden. It is amazing how many things you can do with onions if you take the time to play around with them.

There are few diseases, here in the North at least, that affect onions. I don't have to worry too much about spraying or dusting mine, although I understand that gardeners in the southern states are sometimes troubled by onion maggots.

Parsley

Parsley is an herb that almost everybody knows and likes. There's no need ever to buy any, because it is so easy to grow. I usually start mine in a cold frame or inside on a windowsill. It can stand quite a lot of freezing weather, so it can be transplanted outside very early in the gardening season.

Curled Leaf parsley seems to be the best. This is the type of parsley you would find on your steak in a good restaurant. You don't need to try to grow an awful lot of this; two or three plants in a 2'x2' block will go a long way.

In the fall, you can dig it up, pot it, and bring it inside. Use a good, big pot, as the taproot can be quite long. I have kept parsley plants for as long as a year or two, planting it outside in the spring and bringing it back inside again in the autumn.

Parsnips

Parsnips are grown only for their roots, because the tops are not worth eating. They will grow in practically any soil, but they prefer loose, deep earth. Parsnip seeds are slow to germinate, so don't be discouraged if they don't show up for a while. I like to plant radishes as a companion plant to parsnips in a wide row. As I pull the radishes, I am cultivating the soil around the parsnips at the same time. Parsnips should be thinned so that they are spaced 2 to 3 inches apart.

The quality of parsnips is better after a frost. Leave them in the ground until late fall or early winter. They are at their very best after the ground has been frozen for a while. In fact, one of the best places to store parsnips is right in the garden. Leave some of them in the ground all winter long and dig them up in the spring when you have more space to store them in the root cellar.

I like parsnips and think they are something everyone should consider planting.

Peanuts

Peanuts are easy enough to grow, but they do better in southern states than here in the North because of our shorter growing season. They need about five months of growing time, so take this into consideration when you lay out your garden. You may not have a long enough season where you live. Spanish peanuts can be grown in about 110 days. They bear heavily and take up less garden space than some of the other varieties.

Peanuts thrive in slightly acidic, sandy soil which contains lots of organic matter. A peanut "seed" consists of a hull filled with nuts. These hulls should be planted 1 or 2 inches deep and anywhere from 3 to 6 inches apart. The rows need to be spaced approximately 2½ feet apart.

A peanut plant will produce blossoms and flowers before the stem bends over toward the ground. When it touches the soil, it will root, and a cluster of peanuts will grow there. A mature plant will be 12 to 18 inches tall. When it reaches about two-thirds of its full height, it should be hilled, by pulling dirt up around the stem, or mulched.

Harvest peanuts in the fall, and hang them in an airy shed to dry for a few weeks. Before they are eaten, they should be roasted in an oven at 300°F. for about 20 minutes.

Peas

I suppose that there are people in this world who don't like peas, but I have never met too many of them. Peas are easy enough to grow, but you have to plant a lot of them to get a big harvest. Wide-row planting or block planting are about the only ways to have enough peas, as far as I am concerned. Peas in wide rows tend to hold each other up as they lean one way or the other. The only plants that hit the ground are those on the outside of each row, and, because they are so thickly matted, even they tend to hold themselves upright. Most of the peas will be in the air, dry and easy to get at when harvest time comes around.

You can plant peas in 10-square-foot blocks for big harvests (see directions under Beans, Bush on page 120). Some years, I have planted peas in patches as large as 12 feet square. I am often asked, "How do you get in to harvest them in a patch so large?" Easy. I take a stool, go out in the patch, sit down, reach out for the peas around me, and pick a peck. Then I move the stool and do it again. You may raise so many peas that you can't stay ahead of them!

Peas are a wonderful nitrogen-fixing green-manure crop. After harvest, till the plant residues back into the garden whenever you can. This will help improve the soil. If you have no way to till them in, put them in your compost pile, or save the vines to use as mulch on other plants.

You can sow peas as soon as you can walk in the garden in the spring. They can stand many freezes. In fact, I've had some success planting them in the fall and covering them with mulch. This is a gamble that doesn't always work, but some years I have removed the mulch in the spring and had the peas start to grow as soon as the ground thawed. If you are lucky, you can have an incredibly early crop this way.

Try to plant two or three varieties of peas. Plant some early ones, some midseason ones, and some late ones. You could also try some Sugar Peas. They are so sweet you can eat pods and all. Sugar Snaps grow up to 6 feet tall, so set up a fence or some kind of mesh to support them. Bush varieties of edible-pod peas are also available. They are different from the flat-podded snow peas found in Oriental cooking. Sugar Snaps have become a real favorite over the past ten years.

There are two basic types of peas—the dwarf pea, which will normally grow to be about 26 inches high, and the telephone pea, which will grow higher than 3 feet. The Alderman variety is a good example of a climbing pea. It grows so high that it needs to have some sort of support—like a wire fence.

Try placing a few book matches under pepper plants; the sulfur makes the soil slightly acidic.

There are not too many diseases that affect peas, mainly because they are growing at a time when the weather is quite cool. They should be planted fairly thick—about 2 inches apart. You can be eating early peas nine to ten weeks after you plant them.

Most peas do poorly once the weather warms up. It is a standard rule that the earlier you get them in, the better they will be. But there is one variety you can plant during the hot months; it is called Wando. I like to plant this variety sometime after my earliest lettuce is done. I also plant them in late summer to get a late crop in September. This is right at the height of the weed season, but I almost never have to weed them. I just broadcast the peas in a 1- to 4-foot band and let them grow as I would any cover crop. When the time comes, I harvest the peas and till the plants back under. Planting peas in wide rows helps to keep the soil cool and moist, something peas need if they are to produce in hot weather.

Peppers

Peppers seem to grow much like eggplant. They like a sunny area and soil that is warm, dry, fertile, and slightly acidic. Don't plant them where you have used a lot of lime. There are two basic types of peppers—hot ones and sweet ones. I grow peppers in a wide row, setting the plants 16 inches apart in a 2–1–2 pattern.

People sometimes ask, "How do I grow red peppers?" The answer to that is simple enough. Any pepper will turn red if it is left on the plant long enough. This is true with hot peppers, Hungarian Wax peppers, and even California Wonders.

An old-timer taught me a trick that seems to work pretty well. After the plants have been indoors for six to eight weeks, I set them out in the garden. Before I transplant, I rip three or four matches out of of pocket matchbook and put them in the bottom of the hole where the plant will be set. The peppers seem to enjoy the sulfur in the matches, perhaps because the sulfur lowers the pH of the soil around the roots. If your soil's pH is already low, forget the matches.

Peppers need fertilizer, but they don't like it in large doses. It is a good idea to put compost or manure under them when they are transplanted. Side-dress them with a rich, organic fertilizer when they blossom. Keep insects off with rotenone, if necessary.

I use one other trick. When the plants start to blossom, I take an empty spray bottle and put in a spoonful of Epsom salts—a form of magnesium. I fill the bottle with lukewarm water, shake it, and then spray the mixture right on the leaves of the plants. The leaves turn dark green, and soon I have an abundance of peppers.

Potatoes

Potatoes will grow almost anywhere, but they are happiest in rich, sandy soil. Always try to plant more than one variety. Plant some with your early crops, and some more about a month later. The second planting should be ready in the fall—just in time to put the crop in the root cellar. Your first planting should supply you with small, young potatoes during the summer, but you should not plan to store these.

Potatoes do not like soil that has a high pH. This means you should try to avoid planting them in ground where a lot of lime or wood ashes have been added.

Choose your seed potatoes carefully. Try to get good ones; you only get one chance at growing them. If you buy large seed potatoes, they should be cut into pieces. There should be two to three eyes in each piece. I like to cut up my seed potatoes at least one day before they are going to be planted. This gives the cut surface time to heal over and dry out a little. When I plant them, I put the cut side down. One of the easiest ways to plant potatoes is in trenches about 4 inches deep. Space them at least a foot apart. I put a handful of superphosphate fertilizer and a handful of good rich compost in each space between the potatoes. Superphosphate seems a little safer than a complete fertilizer like 10–10–10. If you do use something like 10–10–10, be sure that none of it touches the seed potatoes. Later on, you can side-dress with a complete fertilizer, as I do. By then there will be no danger of burning the seeds.

When the green tops of the potatoes come up, they should be covered with soil again—leaves and all. (A hoe works best for this.) This is called *hilling*. New potatoes form above the seed you plant, not below it. By building up a hill, you are giving the new potatoes plenty of loose, soft, soil into which they can expand. After you have hilled a couple of times, you should have a long mound, about 8 to 10 inches high, over the row of potatoes. Pay attention to your earlier crop. If you hill it as soon as the green tops show, you will keep the plants protected from frost.

There is an even easier way to plant pota-

Leave two or three eyes in each piece of seed potato.

Hill potatoes as soon as the leaves appear so they'll have loose, soft soil in which to expand.

Seed potatoes can also be broadcast over a plot of tilled ground, then covered with 12 to 18 inches of seed-free mulch. Harvesting will be easy, and your potatoes will be large and clean.

toes—under mulch. This technique is sometimes called *broadcast planting*. Till up an area of soil, say 10 or 12 feet square, and prepare your potato seed just as though you were going to plant them in a furrow. Spread these cut-up seed potatoes right on top of the ground, about 10 inches apart in all directions. You don't have to plant them; just lay them on the surface of the ground.

These seed potatoes should then be covered with 12 to 18 inches of mulch—seed-free mulch, if you have it. That's all! Just forget about them for a while. The tops will grow right up through the hay, and new potatoes will form right on top of the ground beneath the mulch. As the summer goes on, you should reach under the mulch from time to time; if you feel a potato that is big enough to eat, about the size of a golf ball, you can pick it. The first potatoes should be ready just about the time your beans are. Picking early potatoes this way does no harm to the plant.

There are still other advantages to planting potatoes under a mulch. Potato bugs do not seem to venture too far into a mulched potato patch. They will eat some of the plants around the perimeter, but you will see very few of them near the middle. You can walk around the edges and pick off any bugs you see. In the fall, you won't have to dig potatoes; you just rake back the mulch and harvest a whole crop of potatoes just sitting there waiting to be picked.

Two diseases seem to bother potatoes. The first is "late blight" and the second is "common scab." Common scab is encouraged by lime and by ordinary stable manure, so try to keep these out of the potato patch.

When can you harvest potatoes? Pick them whenever they are big enough to eat, as I have already said, but take a little extra care with potatoes that you are going to store. Don't pick them until the tops are dead. There is an easy way to tell a ripe potato from a green one. As soon as you dig it out of the ground, rub the skin with your hand. If the skin rubs off easily, the potato is still green. It is perfectly good to cook and eat this way; it just won't store as well or as long as one that has a tougher skin.

Pumpkins

If you fertilize pumpkins well, they can get to be very big, and they take up a lot of room. It might be best not to plant them unless you have lots of garden space.

If you do decide to grow pumpkins, try to keep them well away from your winter-squash patch, if you want to save the seed. The two plants will cross-pollinate. The seeds produced by the cross-pollinated blossoms may produce some unique and interesting vegetables the next year, but they will not produce "true" varieties. The cross-pollination will not affect this year's crop grown for eating, though.

Plant pumpkin seeds in hills that are at least 8 to 10 feet apart. Once the seedlings come up, the plants should be thinned to four or five per hill. I usually dig a hole beneath the spot where a hill will be and put in a shovelful of manure or compost. Then I sprinkle a little dirt over the top of it and plant the seed. I also plant some radishes to keep the bugs off the pumpkin leaves.

Pumpkins should be harvested when they are fully ripe. They should not be exposed to frost or they will not keep well. When you pick them, be careful not to break off the stem. If you do break one off, use that pumpkin first, because it will be a poor keeper.

You can control the growth of a pumpkin vine. Pick off the fuzzy end of the vine and it will stop growing. This will also help the pumpkins already on the vine to grow larger.

For eating and cooking, we prefer the Baby Sugar pumpkins. One is just right for a pie or mashed for dinner.

I am sure you know or have heard about people who grow pumpkins that weigh 125 to 150 pounds or more. This is not as hard a job as you might think. I have done it many times, even though these huge pumpkins are nearly worthless as far as eating is concerned. To grow a mammoth jack-o'-lantern, dig a big hole and put in about a bushel of aged cow manure mixed with fertilizer. Put a layer of dirt over the manure, and plant three seeds. Big Max is one variety that grows very large. When the seedlings have two or three leaves on them, choose the one that looks the healthiest and pull up the other two. As soon as the vine has grown three small pumpkins, break off its fuzzy end so that it won't grow any farther. Keep an eye on this vine. If new blossoms or small pumpkins start to form, pick them off. Let the plant concentrate on the original three.

When the pumpkins get to be about the size of a man's fist, save the best-shaped one and pick the other two. Let all the strength of the manure go into this single pumpkin. Roll it slightly every once in a while, but not so much that you twist or break the stem. It may have a tendency to flatten out on one side if you don't change its position from time to time.

This is a great project for kids. Before long, they'll be competing to see who can grow the pumpkin that weighs the most. Children will be astonished to find that they can grow something that weighs far more than they do in just a few weeks.

Radishes

Radishes will grow just about anywhere. They don't do quite as well in heavy clay as they do in light, sandy soil because they are a root crop and need room to expand underground. Radishes can be planted as soon as the ground can be worked in the spring, and a second planting will continue to grow late into the fall, even after frost. They will not do especially well in hot weather, so it is best to plant them either early or late. Radishes have a very short maturation time, which means you can plant them many times during the growing season.

To get a really good radish, you should provide fertile soil and encourage quick growth. Those that grow slowly tend to be tough and woody-tasting.

Radishes are a fine companion plant for just about anything else. I plant them with most seeded crops as row markers because they come up in a week or so. They will not harm any other crop. Let the bugs chew on the radish tops. This does not seem to have much effect on the quality of the roots. Harvest the radishes before they get too large, or root maggots may get into them.

Rhubarb

Rhubarb is a very hardy perennial. It does well even in northern states, and it will live for many years. It is best to plant rhubarb roots. You can buy these in a store or send away for them, but the easiest thing is to get some from a neighbor's patch (with permission, of course). Plant rhubarb somewhere out of the way. It will be in place for a long time, so choose a spot where it will not be disturbed. Three or four roots will provide all you can eat.

In the spring, dig a hole and put in some manure or decomposed organic matter. Plant the root in the hole, covering it with about one inch of soil. You will get no harvest from rhubarb the first year, but during this time you should give it lots of fertilizer.

In the second year of growth, the plants will start to put out seedpods. If you keep these cut, the roots will continue to produce tasty stalks all season long. (The large green leaves are poisonous.) The more you harvest, the more the plant will produce.

A rhubarb plant will last ten years or so, but it will demand occasional attention. Every four or five years, in the fall, I drive a shovel right down through the middle of the plant. Then I dig up half of the root. I fill in the hole with manure or compost. This ensures a tender and juicy crop the following year. The half of the plant that I dug up can be saved and planted somewhere else—perhaps in someone else's garden.

I have stored some of these dug-up rhubarb plants in my root cellar. They will do amazing things! One year, I kept some in a box filled with sand and some in a box filled with sawdust. In January, I soaked the sand and the sawdust with water just to see what would happen. When I did, the rhubarb roots sent out little stalks. These looked just like the rhubarb shoots that come up out of the ground in the spring, except that they had no leaves. They looked a little like asparagus shoots. We ate these, and they were a real treat in the dead of winter.

Rutabagas

Rutabagas require exactly the same care as turnips. They grow bigger than turnips and take about a month longer to mature. My favorite rutabaga is the Purple Top variety. I plant rutabagas in a wide row.

Spinach

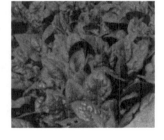

Spinach, although it will grow almost anywhere, prefers cool weather. It should be planted very early—as soon as you can work the soil in the spring. Late March or early April is a good time to sow seed here in Vermont.

Spinach seeds germinate very slowly. Spinach (and any crop that is slow to come

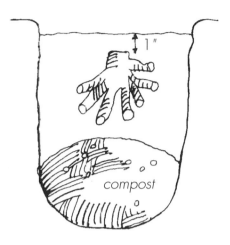

Put plenty of manure or compost under rhubarb roots, and give them lots of fertilizer during their first year.

up) should be marked with radish seeds so that you don't forget the planting and walk on the area by mistake. Once they do appear, spinach plants should be thinned to 2 or 3 inches apart. The faster spinach grows, the more tender it will be and the better it will taste. Fertilizing the soil will help your crop grow faster. If you want large spinach bunches, start your spinach as transplants and then set them out 6 inches apart in 20-inch wide rows.

There are a number of different kinds of spinach. Some varieties are meant to be planted early, and some have been developed for late planting. Take a look at the seed package to learn which is which. My own favorite varieties are Summer Savory, Bloomsdale, and New Viking.

The one bug that bothers spinach is a specialist called the spinach aphid. This is a tiny, yellow-green louse that is easy to discourage with a dusting of rotenone.

Keep leaf crops like spinach harvested. Start picking or cutting it for the table when there are just four or five leaves on each plant. Cut the whole plant down close to the ground, somewhere below the lowest leaf. If you cut it off clean without destroying the stem, it will take the plant much longer to go to seed. If you wait too long before harvesting, hoping that the leaves will get nice and big, you will end up with less spinach in the long run, because the plant will bolt and go to seed very quickly. Once it has done this, it will no longer produce. As soon as three or four new leaves appear after the first cutting, cut the plant back again.

New Zealand spinach is not a true spinach, although the leaves look the same and can be eaten and prepared in the same way as spinach. New Zealand spinach will survive a lot of hot weather, which is a definite advantage. It grows much larger than regular spinach, sometimes getting 2 feet high. It should be planted in rows 3 feet apart with the plants spaced 10 to 12 inches apart after thinning. After five or six weeks it can be harvested, but you should do it a little differently than you would with regular spinach. Leave the center shoot and pick only the side leaves. If you don't injure the center of the plant, it will continue producing for a long time.

Squash

Squash is not a hardy crop, so don't plant it too early. Winter squash, such as the Blue Hubbard, Butternut, Buttercup, and Table Queen varieties, should be planted in hills at least 8 to 10 feet apart. Put four or five seeds in each hill and later thin to three or four plants. One of the sweetest of the winter squashes is a small green-and-white-striped variety called Delicata.

Here in Vermont, at least, we seldom plant winter squash until the first of June, at the earliest. If you wait this long, or even as late as the tenth of June, there will still be enough time to grow plenty of squash and also avoid a lot of bug problems. Planting radishes in each hill is almost a must. They will satisfy a good share of the hungry bugs. Thanks to radishes, I have not had to dust my winter squash for several years.

Summer squash, zucchini, scallop, and cockleshell squash can be planted in hills 3 or 4 feet apart or in rows, placing seeds 8 inches apart. I prefer to plant these squash in single rows, because they take up less room this way. You don't need to plant much summer squash or zucchini to get a big yield. If you do go overboard with it, you won't know what to do with it all and will end up wasting a lot.

Too few people know about harvesting squash buds and blossoms. They are a real delicacy. Pick the buds just before they are about to open into blossoms, just the way you would pick strawberries; then wash them off and sauté them in butter. They are delicious in soups, with meat, or in stews. Squash plants will keep producing buds as long as you keep the fruit harvested. It is easy to gather dozens of squash and many quarts of buds at the same time—a little like having your cake and eating it, too.

Squash will attract aphids and squash bugs, but you already know how to cope with these. Keeping the patch weeded will help to prevent insect problems. If you discover that a squash-vine borer has attacked the main stem of a plant, you can cut out the insect with a knife.

If you then cover the injured part of the stem with soil, it will heal and grow new roots.

Some folks don't seem to know when to harvest squash or what a harvestable squash looks like. I like to use the thumbnail test. When you are selecting a winter squash that you are going to store, for example, push your thumbnail against it as hard as you can. If the outer skin doesn't cut easily, you can be sure that that particular squash will keep for a long time. If it does cut, it probably won't keep so long, but that doesn't mean you can't eat it! It just means that it won't be a good winter keeper. It should be placed near the front of your storage pile, used first, or shared with friends quite soon.

Be sure you leave the stems on your winter squash when you harvest them. If you pull the stem off, the whole squash will rot from that end. If a stem breaks off by accident, use that squash first. Don't wash any vegetables that you plan to store. In fact, handle them as little as possible. The more you handle them, the more likely you are to bruise them. Any blemish on the skin of a squash will cause it to rot more quickly.

Sunflowers

Growing giant sunflowers is a thrill that every gardener should enjoy. As you know, they will grow very, very tall—sometimes as high as 12

FRENCH-FRIED SQUASH

If you'd like to try a new twist with squash, slice them in thin strips and eat them raw in salads or along with an attractive plate of other colorful raw vegetables. Or you can slice yellow squash and fry them just like French-fried potatoes. Children especially love this different treat.

feet or more. If you apply plenty of fertilizer and organic matter when you plant the seed, your sunflowers will grow tall and sturdy. If you want to have early sunflowers, you can start them inside. They are very easy to transplant and can be put right in your corn rows. Sunflowers are one of the few beautiful flowers that produce an edible crop, too. Just remember to plan carefully so that they do not shade other sun-loving crops.

People like sunflower seeds almost as much as birds do, and keeping the birds away can be a problem. As the seeds start to ripen, the heads of the flowers will begin to bend downward. This is the time to tie a piece of plastic mesh (the material of which orange bags are made) around the stem, and wrap it around the seed head. Birds will not put their heads through the mesh to get at the seeds; they will only eat those few seeds that are exposed around the edges.

Harvest sunflower seeds late in the fall. Cut off the head, leaving about 2 feet of stem attached to it. Hang these in some dry place where birds and rodents will not find them. A well-ventilated attic is a nearly perfect place for drying sunflowers. Once the heads are dry, you can remove the seeds by rubbing them off with a stiff brush. You may find the ends of the seeds are still a little damp. If they are, they should be spread out on sheets of newspaper to dry further.

Sweet Potatoes

Sweet potatoes have to be started from plants. This is easy to do and kind of fun. Put a ripe sweet potato in a glass of water. After a few days it will send out a number of small shoots. When these get to be about 6 inches long, pick them off, and put each in another container of water. Leave them there until tiny roots begin to form. Once these roots appear, you can plant the shoots in the garden.

Sweet potatoes are extremely tender. Be sure that you wait until there is no longer any danger of frost before you transplant them. They also need plenty of room. It's best to plant them in long ridges, about 3 feet apart. They like light soil and will require some fertilizer. Sweet potatoes are not bothered by insects very much, so there should be no need to dust.

You can dig sweet potatoes as soon as there is anything big enough to eat. Storing them well is something of a problem—for me at least. To keep really well, they should be put in a very warm and humid place for eight to ten days before they go into the root cellar. I find it easier to can or freeze them.

A neighboring gardener planted the same variety of sweet potatoes at the same time—but on a smaller ridge. When dug, the neighbor's potatoes were as small and round as baseballs. On the high ridge, though, the sweet potatoes grew large and long—up to 29 inches in length.

Swiss Chard

Swiss chard is closely related to the beet, but with chard we are not so much interested in the root. We eat only the leaves.

Swiss chard will produce all summer long. It will stand several freezes, both in the spring and in the fall. Broadcast-seed it in wide rows for best results.

Chard comes in a variety of colors. You can take your choice. The most common type is green. But there is also red chard, called "rhubarb chard," and white chard, which is not really pure white. Many gardeners like the taste of rhubarb chard best, and I can't say that I disagree.

Whichever color you choose, harvest chard like spinach; cut off the entire plant about 1 inch above the ground. Many people make the mistake of picking off only the biggest leaves. These are always the toughest ones. The smaller ones near the center of the plant have the best flavor. Cut down the whole plant and mix the big leaves and the little leaves together. There may be times when your chard will get ahead of you and grow to be a foot tall. When this happens, it is best to mow down the whole row and let the chard start growing all over again.

Tomatoes

Let me tell you my method for planting tomatoes. Because our northern growing season is so short, and because this particular crop takes such a long time to mature, I start my tomatoes indoors about six to eight weeks before the last killing frost. The seeds are planted in shallow pans called flats.

When the seedlings are about 3 inches tall, it is time to transplant them into another flat. I always transplant them deeper than they were growing in the original flat. I leave only the top leaves showing above the soil. All but these uppermost leaves are picked off before transplanting. The buried section of stem begins to grow tiny root hairs. Before long, the stem will have become a tangle of healthy roots capable of supporting a rugged plant. A second transplanting takes place when the plant is about 10 inches tall. I take off all except the very top leaves and set the plant in a 2-quart milk carton, putting the ends of the roots at the very bottom of the carton. By the time these plants are ready to be set out in the garden, they have a stem the size of my little finger and a root structure as deep as the milk carton is tall.

When I get ready to transplant tomatoes into the garden, I dig a 6-inch trench or furrow, put compost or manure into the bottom, then cover that with soil, filling it to within 3 inches of the ground surface. I very carefully take the tomato plant out of the milk carton or flat and lay it down in the trench. Again, I remove all of the leaves except the topmost cluster, even if there are blossoms and small green tomatoes. I cover the entire length of the stem with about 2½ inches of soil and firm it down with my hands. When I get to the leafy end, I support it with one hand and bring soil up underneath it with the other to prop it in a more upright position. Mother Nature will take over the job from there. In no time at all, the plant will have grown straight and tall, and will have developed an extensive and healthy root system.

Because the roots and stem are only 2½ inches below the soil surface, the heat-loving tomato plants get extra warmth early in the season. When the sun comes out and warms the soil, it also warms the roots. A tomato

TRANSPLANTING TOMATOES

When transplanting tomatoes, remove all but the topmost leaves.

Always plant tomato transplants deeper than they were growing before. Only the top leaves should show.

When you transplant a tomato plant to the garden, lay it on its side in the furrow so roots will form all along the stem.

MAKING FRAMES TO SUPPORT YOUR TOMATO PLANTS

Tomato plants can be tied to vertical strings for support.

The "Florida weave" system requires no tying. Run two strings between two (or more) posts and weave the tomato plants in and out of the strings.

A short piece of capped pipe should be placed over the top of tomato stakes before driving them in the ground. This keeps the wood from splitting. Remove the cap and use it to drive next stake.

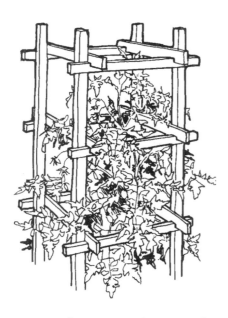

Wooden tomato frames can be reused year after year.

Use concrete reinforcing mesh to make tomato cages. Snip out the bottom rung and push the vertical wires 6 inches into the ground. Wire together loosely so the cages can be unhooked for easy storage.

planted in this way will grow much faster than one planted with its roots deep in the cold earth. Tomatoes should never be mulched until they have been in the ground for about four or five weeks. Mulch insulates the soil and shades it from the sun, so the ground stays cold longer, and this hinders the growth of the plant. Once the soil has warmed up, mulching has certain advantages. For one thing, it will help prevent blossom-end rot by keeping an even moisture content in the soil.

What about staking? The best time to stake

is right after you have transplanted into the garden, so you remember where the underground stem is located. If you wait until later, you might cut the buried stem as you push the stake into the earth. Whenever you stake a tomato—or trellis cucumbers or peas, for that matter—put the support on the downwind side of the plant, so that the prevailing wind blows the plant against the stake or trellis. Otherwise, it will blow against the tie, sometimes hard enough to sever the stem.

When you attach the plant to the stake, use a soft, wide tie. A strip of nylon cloth is better than string, cord, or wire. Tie it tightly around the stake, but loosely and gently around the stem of the plant.

If you decide to stake your tomato plants, keep all of the suckers picked off. Suckers are tiny stems and leaves that grow in the crotches of the larger stems and steal nourishment from the plant. If you decide to let the plants run free along the ground, removing suckers is not quite so important, but you should try to keep at least half of them pinched off.

You can encourage tomatoes to grow on wire or on trellises. If you use tomato stakes, keep tying up the stalk as it grows taller and taller. When it reaches the top of the stake, pick the end off so that the plant will not grow any higher.

A trellis is something that you construct from slats of wood or from wire-mesh fencing. This may seem like a silly thing to say, but if you decide to build a trellis, be sure there is enough room for your hands to get in between the slats or through the wire mesh. The tomatoes may ripen on the inside of the trellis, and there is nothing more aggravating or embarrassing than not being able to get at them when they are ready to pick!

If you use wire, first drive a row of 6-foot

GETTING EARLY TOMATOES

For extra-early tomatoes, one gardener I know selects a few tomato plants after he's set them out and they've got a good start; then he digs them up and transplants them to another spot in the garden. About two weeks later, he transplants them again, being careful to keep some soil around the roots. He finds that these plants bear ripe tomatoes a week to ten days earlier than tomato plants that stay in one spot.

Another way to get earlier tomatoes is to "root prune" them. When the plant has set four or five big clusters of tomatoes, take a long knife and cut into the ground a few inches away from the stem. This will sever part of the root structure, forcing the plant to stop growing and the fruit to ripen early. You can even step on the stem near the ground to partially break it and force early ripening of the fruit. If you have been fertilizing your tomatoes, it may sometimes be necessary to force ripening to stop unwanted growth.

COMPOST BIN TOMATOES

In the summer, you can camouflage your compost bin with tomato plants. Throw in all your leaves, grass clippings, kitchen scraps, and whatever else will rot into the bin, which is made of wire fencing. In the spring, set tomato plants close to the wire all around the bin. As the tomato plants get larger they are tied to the wire "trellis." The roots grow up into the rich compost and provide the plants with the nutrients they need.

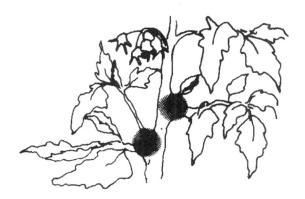

The single-stem method: remove all suckers to prevent the growth of side branches.

stakes firmly into the ground. Between the stakes, string three strands of wire spaced 1 foot apart. The lowest strand should be about 1 foot off the ground. As the tomatoes start to grow, allow them to inter-weave their branches around and through the wires. Let two or three stems grow, and keep the suckers picked off. You may need to tie a stem to one of the wires now and then. Try to encourage them to grow on one side of the first wire, then on the other side of the second, and so forth.

When the tallest branch grows beyond the top wire, pick it off. This will stop the plant from growing any higher. If it grows too far over the upper wire, it will break off anyway. If you don't control its growth, the plant may expend all its energy and use up all its nutrients getting taller and growing new shoots. When this happens, the quality and size of the fruit suffers. Try to get

PRUNING TIPS FOR TOMATOES

Prune a young tomato plant to form a Y-shaped fork low to the ground. Then train the two stalks up a trellis made of string. Tie by looping the cord around the stalk. Don't prune off any more suckers. Keep the vine growing vigorously, so the leaves will shade the tomatoes and protect them from sunburn.

your plants to concentrate more on producing fruit than on growing larger and leafier.

Plant at least two or three varieties; it is risky to rely on just one. What happens, for instance, if there is an early fall frost or an extended drought? One of the varieties of tomatoes will probably survive and provide a crop.

In the fall, as frost approaches, you can harvest the tomatoes that have not ripened yet. The very green ones may never ripen inside, but the whitish ones and the ones that have changed color slightly will. Take them in and set them on a shelf or board. Lay some newspaper over them and check every once in a while to see how they are doing. Turn them over every two or three days so that they don't stay in the same position. You may find that you can keep them for a month or more after the first frost. You can also take in the whole plant and hang it upside-down while the green fruit ripens. Tomatoes should be stored where it is cool and dark.

One of the best varieties is the Pixie. In December, you can plant a Pixie inside the house and by February be harvesting tomatoes from your windowsill. Pixie plants stay quite small and do not grow leggy like other small tomato varieties. If you take good care of your indoor plants, you can grow fruit about the size of golf balls. When spring comes, you can gradually harden the plant off and set it out in the garden. It will seem dormant for a while, but don't be discouraged. Soon you will have some early tomatoes. Pixies, unlike most other tomatoes, will bear fruit throughout the summer. The tomatoes grown outside will be somewhat larger than the ones grown indoors.

There are a lot of things you can do with tomato plants—Pixies or any other type. If you cut two or three suckers from a healthy plant before frost in the fall, stick them in a pot filled with fertile soil, and water them liberally, they will root just like a geranium. You can harvest tomatoes again in December. If you plan carefully, you can grow fresh tomatoes year-round. A 4-quart pot is large enough for most tomato plants. The potting soil should be fertilized with compost, dried manure, or some sort of commercial fertilizer.

Turnips

Turnips should be planted very early in the spring in a wide row. They refuse to do well in hot weather, and they will be happiest in light, fertile soil. An average gardening season should give you two crops—one that matures just as the weather is getting really hot and a fall crop that was planted in midsummer. I usually plant turnips in May and again around the end of July.

Turnip seedlings should be thinned to about 4 to 6 inches apart. They may be threatened by the same diseases and insects that bother members of the cabbage family. You should harvest them like beets and store them the same way, too—in a box of dry sawdust or sand. You will find a lot of insect holes in the leaves sometimes, but these will not affect the quality of the roots.

Watermelons

Watermelons are a lot of fun to grow, but they take a long time and need lots of sun and dry

Pixie Tomato

This compact, sturdy tomato is ideal for growing in a flowerpot or in the garden.

If you've been harvesting from a Pixie all summer, you can extend the season by cutting off a slip or sucker and rooting it in a good potting-soil mixture. Do this around the first of September. When frost threatens, bring it inside and set it in a sunny window. You should have tomatoes by Thanksgiving.

Frozen Raw Tomatoes

Just slice peeled raw tomatoes into a plastic container and freeze them. You can't eat them like fresh tomatoes, but they're fine cooked in meat loaves, spaghetti sauces, soups, and other tomato dishes.

feet. An ideal spot for growing watermelons would slant to the south or west.

Sprout seeds in towels and plant watermelons under hotcaps, just as you would plant any melon. You can use the tin-can trick (see Melons, page 139) once a baby watermelon has grown to be the size of your fist. This helps them ripen faster. Pick off excess blossoms and any fruit that isn't going to have time to mature.

Watermelons are usually planted in hills no closer than 6 to 8 feet apart. Don't cheat them out of the fertilizer they need. Use lots of compost and manure, and give them a good side-dressing of fertilizer at the "stand up" stage (just before the vines are about to run out and away from the center of the plant). Keep checking for shriveled or decayed fruit. You will find some once in a while, but this is no reason to panic. Pick them off immediately, and you will reduce the danger of a disease called "stem-end rot." Watermelons can pick up diseases very easily, so try to stay out of the melon patch when it is wet.

Check the underside of a watermelon to see if it is ripe. If it is still white where it sits on the ground, it is not ready yet. If the underside has begun to turn bright yellow, the melon is ready to be eaten. Toward the end of August, select only those watermelons that you think have a chance of ripening, and pick off all the others. You will get bigger, sweeter melons this way.

SCALING UP:
A STEP BEYOND THE BASICS

I. Energy-Efficient Vegetable Storage

THE PIONEERS who settled this country didn't have deep freezers, but they fed their families all winter long by knowing how to store the harvest from their gardens. If you don't already have a freezer, knowing the old-fashioned ways of vegetable storage will allow you to enjoy your garden well into the winter. I've stored carrots that were still crisp and tasty the following June!

The early settlers often used root cellars for food storage. These were small caves, sometimes dug into a hillside, that kept food in a cool and moist atmosphere. Sometimes they were just part of the cellar, which in old houses provided the same conditions. You can duplicate good vegetable storage conditions without resorting to a cave.

You may choose to freeze or can your harvest, and there's lots of information available in other books on how to do that. But you can also choose to use root cellaring, and this section is devoted to that age-old technique because it is gradually being forgotten—and shouldn't be.

The Basics of Vegetable Storage without Refrigeration

Most fruits and vegetables are between 80 and 95 percent water by weight. When people lose water from their body tissue as vapor it is called *perspiration*. When vegetables lose water as

An abundant garden harvest is not only beautiful and personally satisfying—it also makes good financial sense. Early settlers and people weathering tough economic times like the Great Depression planted enough to carry them through the winter.

- Trim the stems off root crops like carrots, rutabagas, and turnips, so close you include a little of the crop itself. Leave ½ to 1 inch of stem on beets.

- Leave the stems on plants in the squash family and handle them carefully. If the stem comes off, they are likely to rot at the scar; use these vegetables first, since they won't keep well for long.

- Use the "thumbnail test" for squash. Push your thumbnail into the skin. If the skin is hard to break, it is mature and will store well. If the skin breaks easily, use the squash soon—it won't keep well.

- Never wash carrots or potatoes before storing them. Let them dry until the dirt falls off before storing.

- Keep stored potatoes in the dark or they will turn green.

- Never try to store any vegetable or fruit that is damaged or that shows signs of disease or insect activity.

- Treat your root cellar like your garden: shop there first, and then market to supplement what you already have. Use everything up over the winter.

- Before storing onions, dry them outside until the small roots are dry, firm, and wiry-feeling.

vapor it is called *transpiration*.

The basic idea in vegetable storage is preventing or reducing transpiration to prevent wilting. This is done by raising the relative humidity, lowering the air temperature, and reducing air movement in the storage space, and by providing protective packaging. Leafy vegetables such as celery and lettuce tend to lose water quickly, while melons, apples, and squash have less exposed surface and lose water more slowly. You also should consider the vegetable's protective coating. Winter squash has a coat of armor compared to a carrot. Roots stored with the tops attached lose water much faster than those with the tops removed. The exceptions to this rule are the members of the squash family, which should be stored with a piece of the stem attached to prevent decay at the stem scar.

An important thing to remember is that water vapor will move out of vegetable tissues into the surrounding air where there is a difference in humidity of less than 1 percent. The drier the storage air, the more quickly vegetables will wilt.

Storage Containers

To reduce transpiration, some crops should be placed in containers. These can be plastic bags with holes punched in them to allow the crops to "breathe." Kegs and barrels were once widely used. Today, most families have a few coolers sitting around that have to be stored for the winter anyway. One gardener I know moved an old bureau into the root cellar and filled the drawers with dampened peat moss and root crops like carrots, beets, turnips, and rutabagas. Net bags like those onions are sold in are good for storing onions and squash hung up on the rafters.

This big harvest garden measures 30' x 40' and will produce enough for freezing, canning, and root cellaring. A 1,000 to 1,500 square foot garden will yield a tremendous harvest if you grow n wide rows.

The Fall Harvest Season

Storing my fall-picked vegetables is one of my favorite gardening jobs. I like to do most of the work outside on bright, early fall days when the breeze is dry and cool and the sweltering days of summer are already a memory.

Harvesting my storage crops and stocking the root cellar bins and shelves gives me an unmatched sense of satisfaction and security. Once again the earth has been darned good to me and my family, and our hard work has paid off with another winter's supply of wholesome food.

What follows is a roundup of fruits and vegetables that are well suited for storage, along with some old and new tips to help you keep them as long as possible. Remember, there are many factors that can affect your storage success. Some storage techniques may work differently from year to year.

Apples

To keep apples awhile in your root cellar they should be picked when they are mature but not fully ripe. If they're too ripe, they'll break down quickly in storage. Get your storage apples into the root cellar the same day you pick them!

Most apples last longest if they are quite cool, around 32° to 35°F. (0° to 2°C.) with a relative high humidity. Some apples, such as

You don't need to include a window or vent in your root cellar unless it is particularly damp. Be sure to cover any windows with opaque material to keep out all light.

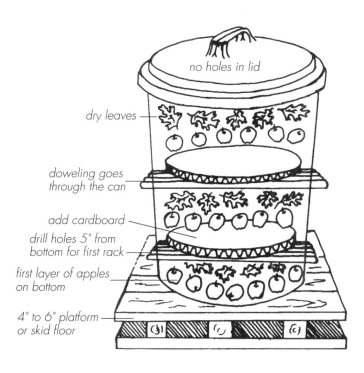

no holes in lid

dry leaves

doweling goes through the can

add cardboard

drill holes 5" from bottom for first rack

first layer of apples on bottom

4" to 6" platform or skid floor

McIntosh, like it a little warmer, around 35° to 40°F (2° to 4.5°C.). Remember that, the higher the temperature, the shorter the storage life.

If some apple skins shrivel slightly in storage, you can firm them up in the kitchen by putting them in a pan of very cold water for a few minutes.

I'd like to share with you one excellent apple-storage system:

Build shelves inside a plastic trash can with doweling and cardboard, and ventilate the structure by drilling holes in the sides of the trash can (see illustration). Then store the can in a cool place that will not freeze.

AN APPLE-STORAGE SYSTEM

1. Drill first series of holes 5 inches up from the bottom of a plastic trash can.

2. Add a single layer of apples.

3. Insert doweling. This provides support for a separation layer.

4. Put cardboard or dry leaves on the dowel racks. Don't fit snugly against the sides of the can, as this cuts down on air circulation. Oak leaves work best for layering.

5. Add another layer of apples, keeping a few inches between compartments.

6. Continue with holes, doweling, cardboard or leaves, and apples to make excellent storage shelves.

Note: Use a trash can lid to cover the can. Put the lid on snugly, but do not drill any holes in it. Also, keep the entire can raised 4 to 6 inches off the floor.

Beets

Large beets keep a little longer than smaller, bunch-sized beets, so if you've got a lot of beets and a few extra minutes, it might pay to sort them for size before bagging them up for storage.

Remember to keep ½ to 1 inch of tops on your beets. You don't want to cut too close to the neck, because the beets could "bleed." On the other hand, leaving too much top causes them to lose moisture more quickly than they should. Store beets the same way as carrots (see Carrots entry, next page).

Beets seem to like a lot of humidity in the storage cellar. As with many other root vegetables, the temperature should stay between 32° and 45°F. (0° and 7°C.) for sound keeping. The closer the temperature is to 32°F., the better it is for your beets.

Cabbages

Cabbages seem to be the fussiest keepers for gardeners who store them for the first time, and for gardeners who live in central and southern areas. A winter warm spell in these regions can mean trouble for stored heads. (If they start to go by, you'll soon get a sniff of a three-alarm odor!) Here are some tips to help you avoid any problems:

- ❦ Keep the crop in the garden as long as you can before cutting and storing cabbages. They'll take a couple of frosts out there.
- ❦ Store only solid heads from your *late* crop, and don't bump or bruise them in transit.
- ❦ Cut off bottom stems and loose outer leaves. (Leaves interfere with important ventilation in storage.)
- ❦ Wrap each head in 10 or 12 layers of

Beets are among the many crops that can be root cellared over the winter. Remove the dirt, but don't wash them, and cut off the greens, leaving just an inch of stem to prevent bleeding. Store them in containers of moist sand or peat moss in a cool space in the cellar. Beets, carrots, and turnips will also store well in plastic bags with holes punched in them for ventilation. You can even stack vegetables in a foam cooler lined with newspaper. Include an open jar of water and refill the jar as needed.

newspaper fastened with a rubber band.
- ❦ Store in plastic bags that have a few holes punched in them.
- ❦ Store heads where it's cold—32° to 35°F. (0° to 2°C.) is ideal. I put cabbages on the lowest shelves of the root cellar.
- ❦ Cabbage wilts quickly in dry storage; keep the humidity high.

If you're storing cabbage heads outside in pits or buried containers, remember: heads must not freeze. (Farmers in the South used to run tillers and plows down between the rows to raise soil up over cabbage heads when freezing weather came. This insulated the heads from freezing.)

If you do have difficulty with storage, keep growing cabbages but use them early in relishes or sauerkraut or pickle them. My wife Jan is using part of this year's storage crop to test some pickled cabbage recipes! Cabbage wedges also freeze very well.

Carrots

Never wash carrots before storing them or they will spoil. After pulling or digging them up, cut off all the greens very close to the carrot itself. Don't be afraid to take a little of the carrot itself. (Treat rutabagas and turnips the same way.) Let the carrots dry for an hour or two and rub off any large clumps of dirt. Set aside any bruised or damaged carrots for early use.

For the past few seasons I've had great luck keeping the carrots in a large white plastic bag on the floor of the root cellar. I poke a few holes through the bag and leave it open a little at the top to allow excess moisture to escape.

You can also pack carrots in cardboard boxes or crates between layers of sand, soil, peat moss, or sawdust.

Carrots can be stored right in the garden throughout the winter. Put on a very thick layer of mulch—up to 18 inches in the Far North—and extend it a foot or more to each side of the row. You can pull fresh carrots out from underneath the snow and mulch all winter long. Be sure to remulch the bed thoroughly after each winter harvest. Dig only

what you can eat within a few days. Carrots will not keep long after digging.

Celery

Celery keeps pretty well, but, just as with growing, the plants need some extra attention in storage. I like to harvest celery before the first hard freezes of fall, keeping the roots and soil attached. I pack the plants in a shallow box of moist soil or sawdust and put them on the floor of the root cellar.

Celery likes temperatures as close to 32°F. (0°C.) as possible. It's important to keep the tops of the plants dry. To keep the plants from wilting, a high humidity level in the storage area is necessary. If you think the air in your root cellar is too dry, spread some burlap on the floor and keep it moist. This helps to raise the humidity.

Horseradish

I harvest horseradish in both the spring and the fall. Wait until after a couple of good freezes and then dig up part of your row. Store only healthy roots and toss out those with bruises or shovel wounds.

Store horseradish roots like carrots. Often, I put some roots on a tray and flash-freeze them. Then I store them in plastic bags in the freezer. Grind horseradish immediately after thawing to preserve its flavor.

Onions

Onions are sorted for size at my place. We pull them, let them dry outside for a day or so, and then sort and cure them by size. A long curing in a warm, airy place gets rid of excess moisture that would cause rot in storage. I usually hang mesh bags of onions (and shallots and garlic, too) in my carport out of direct sun for three or four weeks to get this curing job done.

Mild or Bermuda types of onions aren't the best keepers, so we plan on using them first, either fresh, in soups, or frozen. The harder yellow types such as Ebenezer, Yellow Globe, and hard yellow Spanish varieties are the mainstay of our onion crop for storage.

Onions need low temperatures and good air circulation. I use various-sized mesh bags for onions and hang them up in the root cellar.

I heard last year from one gardener who accidentally left a big bag of onions on his back porch, where they froze solid over the winter. He was surprised in the spring when the onions thawed out and were A-OK. Well, he was just lucky. Freezing usually means serious trouble for onions (and most other stored vegetables), but sometimes, if they thaw out very slowly with no handling at all, they will make it. If they do freeze and thaw, use them right away, since they won't keep very long.

Parsnips

Parsnips will stand a little frost, but they don't like alternate freezing and thawing. Pack them in sand, sawdust, or peat moss and store them on the floor of the root cellar. Keeping the material moistened is important.

You can also leave parsnips in the ground over the winter and dig them up for use in the spring. Freezing will not hurt them.

Potatoes

Darkness, cool temperatures (35° to 45°F.—2° to 7°C.), and good air circulation are the keys to good potato storage in the home. Just a small

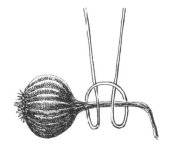

BRAIDING ONIONS

Loop string around onion top.

Braid in second onion as shown.

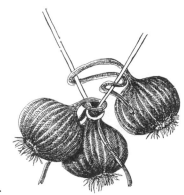

Repeat with third onion and others.

amount of light will gradually cause greening of the potatoes. A common error is storing them in burlap bags in a lighted area. The light actually penetrates the burlap and greens the outer potatoes.

To promote air flow around potatoes, I put them only 12 to 18 inches deep in bins with *slatted* sides and bottoms. I also keep the bins at least 3 inches off the floor. Since there's constant movement of water from inside the

Our basement root cellar contains things we pickle and can as well as a variety of crops that are stored just as they were harvested. We "shop first in the garden" in summer and "shop first in the root cellar" in winter.

potato to the outer surface of the skin, the air flow is important to carry off this moisture and reduce the chances for rotting.

At storage time I like to gently sort out potatoes by size. Jan gets the very small ones. She puts them through a hand-cranked peeler and cans quite a few. A few of the "football"-size spuds are placed on the top of the bins for bragging rights!

Most mature potatoes (your thumb can't rub off any skin on these) will keep quite a while at most any temperature. But the warmer it is, the sooner the potato will sprout and start to break down.

Pumpkins and Winter Squash

The old-timers around this part of the country used to store pumpkins and winter squash under their beds. The practice may become popular again as people turn the thermostat way down in the bedroom to save energy. Squashes don't need the very cool temperatures that other vegetables such as root crops and potatoes need. Around 50° to 55°F. (10° to 13°C.) is fine. In the root cellar, they can go in bags hung from the ceiling or on shelves that are chest- or waist-high. Wiping squash and pumpkins with a solution of 1 cup bleach in 1 gallon of water kills some of the bacteria and improves storage life. Don't rinse the squash before storing, but scrub the skin before cooking. Winter squash can also be cooked and frozen.

Rutabagas and Turnips

Like carrots and beets, these crops keep well in ventilated plastic bags where the temperature is cool (32° to 45°F.—0° to 7°C.) and where there is high humidity.

You can coat rutabagas and turnips with hot paraffin wax to help keep them from losing moisture and weight. We used to do this at home, but found that in our root cellar, which stays quite cool, turnips and rutabagas keep just as well in plastic bags without waxing.

If you want to try waxing, buy $1 or $2 worth of paraffin. Carefully wash the crop and dry and cool all the turnips and rutabagas you're waxing. Melt the wax down over heat, and keep it hot. Then dip each vegetable into the wax, quickly submerging it or rolling it quickly in the liquid. Try for a thin layer of wax, since too much wax actually traps moisture and gasses and shortens storage life.

Sweet Potatoes

Sweet potatoes must be pampered come harvest time. They don't like cold temperatures or wet soil just before harvest. If they get nipped by cold they don't store or cook up as well.

Down South, sweet potatoes are cured indoors for a week or so after digging for the best storage. The curing temperature must be high: near 85°F. (30°C.) is best, with fairly high humidity. This heals over injuries and bruises from digging and handling them. The lower the temperature, the slower and less effective the healing.

Once cured, sweet potatoes are best kept in temperatures of 55° to 60°F. (12° to 16°C.), just like winter squash. If it gets much cooler than 55°F., the sweet potatoes start to break down.

Up North we don't have a long enough growing season to grow the very big, good-keeping sweet potatoes. So we cook and freeze most of the harvest right at digging time and save a lot of time and worry about curing and the cool temperatures in our root cellar. Jan

likes to bake sweet potatoes in 1½-inch-thick slices and then freeze them.

Here's another method of baking and freezing sweet potatoes: trim the potatoes, bake them in their skins, cool them, and then wrap each one individually in foil for freezing. Planning ahead for sweet potato pies, you can scoop the meat out of a number of cooked potatoes and pack it separately in containers for freezing.

Tomatoes

Green tomatoes that have started to turn color can be stored and ripened in your root cellar or any other dark place. An old bureau drawer makes a great ripening chamber. They will ripen in a dark area at temperatures between 55° and 70°F. (13° and 21°C.). Putting them on a windowsill will turn them red, but tomatoes ripen from the inside out, so they might not ripen to full flavor.

To ripen in storage, spread the tomatoes out on a shelf and cover them all with a sheet or two of newspaper. This traps the ethylene gas that tomatoes give off and speeds their ripening.

If you have a choice, the best tomatoes to bring indoors to ripen are those from plants that are in the early stages of bearing. This is because older plants get sort of tired at the end of the season, and the quality of their fruit is apt to be inferior. The longest keepers will usually last from four to six weeks.

Zucchini

Large, overgrown zucchini will keep for a couple of months in the root cellar. Leave an inch or so of stem attached. Peel off the thick outer skin before cooking.

II. Building Soil with Green Manures

If your soil has been neglected for many years, it will most likely take more than one year to restore it to a productive, fertile state. Nature does things gradually, but there are some things that the gardener can do to create ideal conditions and give nature a boost.

Growing green manures is an outstanding technique for improving soil texture by increasing its humus content and building up the available supply of topsoil plant nutrients. Plants grow by drawing nutrients from the soil, die, and then return to the earth those nutrients that were used in growing. Green manures are crops grown simply for the purpose of being chopped and mixed directly back into the soil.

Seven Reasons for Growing Green Manures

1. With green manuring, you can avoid the time and work of collecting and hauling organic matter to your garden.
2. Green manure is a very economical source of organic matter.
3. Once a green manure crop has been turned under, it provides excellent food for earthworms.
4. The roots of many green manure crops reach deep into the subsoil, absorbing valuable nutrients and bringing them up into the plant tissues. When the crop is turned under, these nutrients will revitalize the topsoil.
5. Certain crops, called *legumes*, can capture and fix large amounts of nitrogen from the air. Legumes add more of this important plant nutrient to the soil when tilled under than they consumed in growing.
6. Depending upon your specific soil profile, growing green manures can cut down on your need to purchase fertilizers and other soil additives and conditioners.
7. A green manure garden becomes more and more weed-free every year because the crops choke out weeds.

Nitrogen Content of Green Manures

Most impressive of all is the evidence that agricultural experiment stations have turned up on the actual fertilizing qualities of various green manures. They produce a broad range of minerals for enrichment of the soil. They are a particularly good source of nitrogen, which is essential to plant growth. The box on the next page gives rough percentages of nitrogen (N) on a dry basis for some crops.

Summarizing many experiments with corn, the USDA reports that a good growth of a winter legume turned under three to four weeks before planting corn will produce as much corn per acre as 50 to 100 pounds of commercial nitrogen. If you use nitrate of soda, a common nitrogenous fertilizer, a good green manure crop can benefit your corn as much as 250 to 500 pounds of this fertilizer.

An effective green manuring program can reduce by about one-half the fertilizer needs of the average garden.

Sowing a Green Manure Crop

You can sow an appropriate green manure crop at any time during the growing season, but if you want to raise green manure and vegetable crops in the same spot during the same year, you should embark on a green manure plan in late summer.

If you have plenty of land, perhaps you'll want to grow food crops in one part of your garden and begin improving another part with green manures. Each year, you could rotate your food crops and green manures. This would be ideal, but most gardeners don't have the luxury of having so much space.

Here's how to proceed if you can't rotate your garden spots. All garden residues should go back into the soil before you sow a green manure crop. Turn under those residues when they're still green—the sooner after harvest the better. They're more succulent to the earthworms and microbes at that time, and they break down much faster. You can get a jump on green manuring by sowing seeds between the rows after your final fall cultivation. Later, you can turn under the crop residues and some green manure.

If you have a rear-end rototiller, it's very easy to turn under all kinds of residues—tomato and pea vines, thick roots, even standing cornstalks. Cutting down garden plants and weeds with a rotary mower will make it possible for you to incorporate organic matter with any good tiller or garden tractor. If you are gardening by hand, without power equipment, you may want to reduce your garden residues in a compost pile. The tough fibers will be at least partially broken down during the composting process—enough to make the work of spading under by hand more manageable.

NITROGEN CONTENT

Crop	Percentage of N
Alfalfa	3.0-4.0
Vetch, hairy	3.0-4.0
Austrian winter peas	3.0-3.8
Clover, crimson	3.0-3.3
Clover, red	2.8-3.2
Cowpeas	2.5-3.0
Lespedeza, common	2.2-2.5
Lespedeza, sericea	2.1-2.4
Lupine, blue	2.0-2.5
Oats	1.3-1.4
Rye, winter	1.2-1.3
Ryegrass	1.2-1.3

All but the last three are legumes. Note the higher percentage of nitrogen of these legume crops.

Preparing the Seedbed

After your garden is clear of crop residues, you are ready to prepare a fall seedbed. Most green manure seeds are on the small side, so the seedbed should be groomed fine. This will speed germination and get the crop off to a fast start.

If you didn't get a chance to add some ground limestone last spring, now is a good time to do so. A soil test is one way to judge more accurately the amount needed. Lime will not interfere with the germination of the green manure seeds you're about to plant. The lime can be lightly broadcast by hand, then tilled or turned into the topsoil.

One of the disadvantages of using chemical fertilizer is that it sometimes overstimulates foliage and green growth in food crops at the expense of the fruit. Don't worry about this with green manures. Stimulating green growth is exactly what you want to do. Especially if you've had a very poor gardening season on neglected soil, you should apply a generous amount of 10–10–10 fertilizer before planting green manure. This will boost the growth of the crop and will ensure an ample harvest of organic matter. You can spread and till in the fertilizer at the same time you apply the ground limestone.

Sowing the Seed

The easiest way to sow the seeds of your green manure crop is by hand, broadcast-style. Just make sure you don't get heavy-handed and sow too thickly; your crop will grow faster if the plants are spaced far enough apart.

Next, the seed should be lightly covered with fine soil. This can be done with a rear-end rotary tiller or by hand with a rake, just as you would if you were planting a new lawn. Most grains, such as wheat, oats, and buckwheat, should be covered to a depth of 1 inch.

Smaller seeds, such as the clovers, need only be covered by ½ inch of soil. Firming in the seed by walking over the seedbed or by rolling will hasten germination, as will watering if conditions are dry.

Up and Growing

In a few weeks, a green manure crop of ryegrass will form a light green blanket of grass and roots, which will benefit your garden, even if it only grows a few inches before winter sets in. The tight web of roots will hold the soil securely and stop erosion that could result from wind and rain. It will also prevent needless evaporation of moisture from uncovered soil.

The next spring, a thick matting of dead (annual) ryegrass will be all ready to chop up and spade or till under, once the soil has warmed up sufficiently. Already the dead and decomposing grass and roots are providing food for the earthworms.

If you used a perennial crop, such as a rye that survives the winter, you should allow it to grow up again in the spring before tilling it under, in order to get a double helping of organic matter. Since it's best to till under any kind of organic material ten days to two weeks before planting, the area in which a perennial green manure was grown will have to be reserved for a late-planted crop, such as sweet corn or tomatoes.

The Most Popular Green Manure Crops for Home Use

Ryegrass

The hardy one with lush, rapid, green growth, ryegrass is easy to grow and yields abundant organic matter. It will take hold in almost any soil anywhere in the country. The seed is easy to find in farm-supply stores. For most purposes, I recommend the annual type, which will survive only until the heavy freezes of winter. It's ideal for the early section of the garden; by the next spring, the grass and roots will be dead, partially decomposed, and easy to turn under.

If you plant the perennial or permanent variety of rye grass, called winter rye, it can survive the winter and yield another harvest of green growth in the spring. Tilling it under will completely shred and bury the roots so they won't return to interfere with your next crop.

Buckwheat

It's hard to beat buckwheat as a green manure for impoverished soil. It will grow in sand, clay, and overly dry or wet areas. Of course, it will be scraggly and reflect the poor soil quality, but at least you can get a cover crop growing. Buckwheat can be broadcast by hand.

Like rye, buckwheat produces a lot of organic material very quickly. It's especially good for loosening up tough sod and killing weeds and lawn grasses when you're making a brand-new garden.

Buckwheat is much hardier than most of the other grains, such as wheat, corn, and oats. It does particularly well in the Northeast, but

OATS AS A COVER CROP

If you use oats for a cover crop, plant early in the spring to give the plants time to "stool," which means that a cluster of stalks will grow up from one root clump. You will get more growth from a smaller amount of seed planted.

RYEGRASS ROOTS

One rye plant can grow an estimated *three miles* of roots—in just one day! In one year, it will produce a total of 387 miles of roots. The plants are continually building underground compost piles. In a one-half-acre garden, a crop of rye will produce 400 to 800 pounds of root growth, all of which will decompose and add humus to the soil.

don't hesitate to try it in other sections of the country.

Buckwheat is actually a summer green manure. It's best to sow it when the ground is thoroughly warmed in summertime, say in June or July, after you've harvested your peas and other early crops. It will reach the blossom stage in about six or eight weeks and will be ready for harvesting as a mulch, as chicken feed, or—a little later when seeds are fully mature—for making your own buckwheat flour.

You'll usually find honeybees swarming through buckwheat blossoms. Pollen is often hard to find at that time of year, and the bees absolutely love it. It makes a rich, dark, flavorful honey.

In late summer, a rear-end rotary tiller can be used to chop up and turn under a hip-high growth of buckwheat. A better alternative to turning under your buckwheat crop is to mow it down and leave it. The seeds will settle in the loosened soil and replant the crop the following spring. This way, you can get two green manure crops from a single sowing if your soil really needs improvement and if you can wait that long before planting a food crop. To get rid of buckwheat permanently, be sure to till it under after it blossoms but before the seeds develop.

As you gain experience and your garden grows you should begin a long-range program of soil building using green manures. One of my favorites is buckwheat, which easily tills into the soil. A garden that is not being used for a season should be planted with a green manure crop to keep out weeds and to build the soil while it is resting.

Legumes

Legumes have a very special importance when used for soil improvement. They attract certain types of soil microbes to their roots; these microbes extract nitrogen from the air and convert it into a form usable by the plants. So a legume actually returns more nitrogen to the soil than it used in growing.

To make sure that nitrogen-fixing microbes are present, it's usually recommended that you inoculate legume seeds with a mixture of these tiny creatures before planting. The inoculant culture, which comes as a dark powder, can be purchased from most suppliers of legume seeds. Mix the inoculant with water according to the directions and evenly coat the seeds.

Clover is the best-known legume. There are many kinds of perennial clovers, so there is most likely one well suited to your climate. The blossoms are ideal for honeybees. With both vetch and clover, you should plan to allow the crop to grow at least one full season, perhaps two, to get the maximum benefit from nitrogen fixation and green growth. Alsike clover has the benefit of growing on ground too wet for the red clovers. One disadvantage of vetch and clover, however, is that they're wiry and sometimes difficult to destroy completely if left for several years.

Hairy vetch, one of the many types of vetch, is perennial but relatively slow-growing. It's good to plant a fast-growing annual "nurse crop" like rye or oats along with the inoculated vetch seed to provide shade and check competitive weed growth. Rye also gives support to the vinelike growth of vetch. If you do decide to plant two crops at once, plant the perennial more thinly than you would ordinarily. Otherwise, the annual nurse crop may be choked out.

Many common vegetables are legumes, so you can get both food and green manure from the same crop. All members of the bean and pea family are legumes. As you have probably discovered, it takes a large planting of garden peas to provide enough for your family. They're so delicious that they don't go far. Well, you can really stretch your pea harvest and get many of the beneficial effects of a cover crop by broadcasting the seeds in very wide rows. This way, they'll choke out competitive weeds and keep the ground moist and cool, too.

You can get away with thick plantings of peas in most soils because they're so hardy. And, as legumes, they produce helpful amounts of nitrogen.

Cowpeas are a fast-growing crop excellent for use as green manure because they produce so much foliage. Try sowing them in combination with oats to help support the vines.

Another good edible legume is the common soybean, which is becoming increasingly important as a true meat substitute. Soybeans are the only vegetable which have the essential proteins of meat. A crop of soybeans can, of course, be grown strictly as a green manure. They will greatly improve the soil in just one season.

Alfalfa

From all the research we've done, it seems that alfalfa is Number One when it comes to green manures. American farmers and gardeners realize the value of this legume. It is estimated that over one-third of all the hay produced in our country is now alfalfa.

Alfalfa is right on top in terms of protein content, which breaks down into usable nitrate "fertilizer." It's one of the most palatable and nutritious foods for livestock, so it must be a delicacy for earthworms, too!

If you'd like to take advantage of this fertile green manure, you can either plant alfalfa and let it grow for at least two seasons in a section of your garden, or you can grow it in a permanent spot nearby and harvest it as mulch. More than one season is needed for its roots to reach their full length—up to 20 feet.

Alfalfa's nitrogen content is considerably higher than that of most legumes. Its leaves and stalks store up many more nutrients than they use in growing. Alfalfa also contains calcium, magnesium, phosphorus, potassium, manganese, and zinc, which makes it a nearly complete natural fertilizer.

Weeds

Weeds—a green manure crop? Yes! These guardians of the soil must not be overlooked. They are Mother Nature's most common green manure. Weeds help to correct for nutrient and trace-mineral imbalances in a soil. Most weeds are very deep-rooted and draw valuable elements up to the topsoil. We think of them as a nuisance because they compete with other crops, but in that idle section of your garden, they're busily at work, if only keeping the topsoil covered and intact. Just be sure to till them under before they go to seed, especially if you intend to plant food crops in that spot next year.

Kale

A lot of people have never tasted freshly picked kale. It happens to be an amazing crop for a lot of reasons. It's very easy to grow; bugs don't bother it much; you can plant it anytime from early spring to late fall; and it can be sown as a green manure crop. It does everything for your soil that a good, thick, nonleguminous green manure crop should do. Frost only improves the flavor of kale; you can actually dig it out of the snow in the dead of winter. Kale can be picked anytime to provide delicious greens for cooking like spinach or for serving raw in salads. It's also extremely high in vitamin A.

Plant Green Manures All Season for Maximum Results

Once you see the improvement that comes from green manuring, you'll try not to let bare parts of your garden waste valuable growing time again. A few weeks after turning under the residues of your early crops, like peas and lettuce, you can start your green manure program. Broad strips of annual ryegrass can get a head start in midsummer, well before the onions and other nearby vegetables are harvested.

Spring. If you'd like to plant a green manure in very early spring to improve soil that will be planted later in the season, try garden peas of an early variety. They produce rapid growth in great quantity and can be planted as soon as the soil can be worked in the spring. After you harvest the peas and turn under the residues as green manure, wait a week or so, then plant your next food or green manure crop.

Summer. For growing in midseason, I recommend buckwheat. It thrives in dry, hot summer weather because its dense clusters of stems shade and cool the ground. Oats are good, too, if moisture is sufficient, and they're always easy to buy.

Fall. Rye is the ideal fall crop because of its hardiness. You can even plant it in late October, if the weather remains mild, and still get a few inches of green growth. The perennial winter rye will survive and shoot up again in the spring, allowing gardeners in the warmer climate zones to grow up to four full green manure crops in one year.

A Perpetual-Yield Garden

Can there be such a thing as a garden that yields forever without having artificial fertilizer added to it? The answer to this question is not clear, but it is something that we should be trying to find out. I have been so concerned about the possibility of a worldwide fertilizer shortage that I have been doing a little experimenting on my own large garden.

I am trying to grow vegetables on individual test plots without adding any chemical fertilizer, manure, or organic matter that was not grown right on the garden plot itself. I do this by rotating vegetables and various cover crops and by tilling the residues from all crops right back into the soil. The only things that I have added to these plots are lime and some trace minerals which the soil was lacking to begin with.

I rotate the cover crops from one year to the next. I plant annual ryegrass, peas, beans, and vegetable crops. I have been doing this with great success for several years now, but I am not sure how long it can be maintained. I have, though, been able to grow tremendous cover crops and vegetable crops, apparently without depleting the soil.

The first year, I grow vegetables on one half of the plot, and plant early peas followed by beans on the other half. As soon as they have been harvested and the residue tilled back into the soil, I plant annual rye and leave it in place until the spring of the following year. The second spring, I rotate the crops. I plant vegetables where the peas and beans had been, and peas and beans where the vegetables had been.

On other plots, I have vegetables one year, and then green manure crops for the next two years. This technique obviously adds a great deal more organic matter to the soil, but I am not sure if it is better than the other method. You should try some similar experiments yourself. It will improve your soil. You will be killing weeds, adding organic matter, and encouraging a large population of earthworms.

YOUR CUSTOMIZED CHART FOR PLANNING AND PLANTING

(Copy these pages for year-to-year record keeping. Sketch your garden on the back.)

Annual Vegetable	Amount to plant per person	Feet of row per person		Plants/ft. after thinning* or transplants/ft.		Distance between plants	Width of wide row
		Single row	Wide row	Single row	Wide row		
HARDY CROPS		*(Plant when ground can be worked, 20–40 days before the last frost.)*					
BROCCOLI	5-10 plants	8-12'	4-6'	1	5	12-14" stagger planting 2-1-2	16"
BRUSSELS SPROUTS	5-10 plants	8-12'	4-6'	1	5	12-14" stagger planting 2-1-2	16"
CABBAGE	5-10 plants	8-12'	3-6'	1	5	12-14" stagger planting 2-1-2	16"
GARLIC	5 bulbs	2'	1'	3-4	36	3-4"	20"
KALE	¼ pkt.	5-10'	3-6'	3*	9	6-8"	16"
KOHLRABI	¼ pkt.	3-5'	1-3'	3-4*	24*	3-4"	16"
ONION SETS	1 lb.	10-15'	3-6'	6	49	2-3"	20"
ONION PLANTS	1 bunch	10-15'	3-6'	6	36	3-4"	20"
PEAS	¼ lb.	15-25'	6-12'	6-7	24	2-4"	16–36"

* These are plants started by sprinkling seeds in the row and then thinning by hand or by dragging a garden rake through the row. Peas and beans are easier to seed by hand and do not need thinning. The numbers per row are approximate for all small seeds. Remember, they do need room to grow.

YEAR_____				
Average last frost date in spring:_____		**Average first frost date in fall:_____**		
Varieties planted and "sure crop" recommendations	**Date Planted**	**Date of First Harvest**	**Succession crop and date**	**Comments**
DeCicco			No — smaller heads will form after first central head is harvested.	Best started from transplants; seeds require 80–100 days to harvest.
Jade Cross			No	Best started from transplants; requires 100+ days from seed. Pick off lower leaves after sprouts form.
Late Flat Dutch			No — cut first head and smaller heads will form.	Transplants best.
Cook's Favorite				Start harvesting when small. Use tops and bulbs.
Dwarf Curled			Midsummer	Will survive frost, snow.
White Vienna			Late summer	Best at 3" in diameter. Substitute for water chestnuts in stir-fry.
Southport Yellow; Ebenezer			Follow early harvest with additional sets.	Use fresh from greentails to maturity. Harvest for storage after tops fall over.
Spanish Yellow			No	
Little Marvel; Patriot; Sugar Snap; Wando			Follow with fall crops such as seeded cauliflower, turnips, kohlrabi, broccoli.	Does well in spring. Doesn't like hot weather. Sugar Snap varieties require 5–6' fence or poles.
NOTES:				

YOUR CUSTOMIZED CHART FOR PLANNING AND PLANTING

Annual Vegetable	Amount to plant per person	Feet of row per person		Plants/ft. after thinning* or transplants/ft.		Distance between plants	Width of wide row
		Single row	Wide row	Single row	Wide row		
RADISH	½ pkt.	5-10'	2-4'	10*	140*	1-2"	16"
RUTABAGA	½ pkt.	5-10'	2-5'	2-3	10-12	6-8"	16"
SHALLOTS	5 bulbs	2'	1'	3-4	24	4-5"	20"
SPINACH	½ pkt.	5-10'	2-5'	4-5*	20*	3-5"	16"
TURNIP	¼ oz.	10-15'	2-5'	3-5*	10-12*	6-8"	16"
SEMI-HARDY CROPS	*(Plant 10-30 days before last frost.)*						
BEETS	½ pkt.	5-10'	3-6'	6-8*	30*	2-4"	16"
CARROTS	½ pkt.	5-10'	3-6'	7*	50*	1-2"	16"
CAULIFLOWER	3-5 plants	5-10'	3-6'	1-2	9	8-10" stagger planting	20"
LETTUCE	½ pkt.	5-10'	2-4'	Head, 2-3; Leaf, 5-6	Head, 9* Leaf, 20*	Head, 8-10" stagger planting; Leaf, 4-5"	16"
SWISS CHARD	¼ pkt.	5-10'	2-4'	5-6*	20*	4-6"	16"

* These are plants started by sprinkling seeds in the row and then thinning by hand or by dragging a garden rake through the row. Peas and beans are easier to seed by hand and do not need thinning. The numbers per row are approximate for all small seeds. Remember, they do need room to grow.

YEAR_____

Average last frost date in spring:_____   **Average first frost date in fall:_____**

Varieties planted and "sure crop" recommendations	Date Planted	Date of First Harvest	Succession crop and date	Comments
Cherry Belle			Plant at two-week intervals	Plant with other seeds to mark rows.
Purple Top			No	Good for winter storage.
			Follow with second crop of lettuce.	Onionlike; used in French sauces or fresh.
Bloomsdale Long-Standing			Plant and harvest early. Follow with most tender crops.	Likes cool weather. Goes to seed quickly in warm weather.
Purple Top			Follow early harvest with fall salad greens or peas.	Good for winter storage.
Detroit Dark Red			Midsummer	Beet greens removed during thinning can be cooked like other greens.
Nantes Half Long			Midsummer	Darkest green foliage indicates the largest carrots.
Early White			Late summer	Start as transplants in spring. Seed in early summer for fall crops.
Leaf: Dark Green. Boston Loosehead: Buttercrunch; Ithaca			Early and late summer	3" spacing for leaf lettuce, 8" for head lettuce. Cut, don't pull, for second and third harvest.
Fordhook; Ruby Chard			Cut in all seasons.	Cut and serve when plants are 8-10" tall.

NOTES:

YOUR CUSTOMIZED CHART FOR PLANNING AND PLANTING

Annual Vegetable	Amount to plant per person	Feet of row per person		Plants /ft. after thinning* or transplants/ft.		Distance between plants	Width of wide row
		Single row	Wide row	Single row	Wide row		
TENDER VEGETABLES		*(Plant on the average last frost date.)*					
SNAP BEANS (bush)	½ lb.	25-50'	10-15'	6-8	20	3-4"	20"
SNAP BEANS (pole)	¼ lb.	15-25'	No	4-6	4-6	4-6 seeds per pole; 6" apart in a row.	6"
LIMA BEANS	¼ lb.	10-15'	8-10'	5-8*	16*	3-6"	16"
CANTALOUPE	½ pkt.	2-3 hills	2-3 hills	3-6 per hill	No	4-6' between hills / 4-6' between rows	
SWEET CORN	½ lb.	25-50'	No	4-6	No	8-12" between plants / 30-36" between rows	
CUCUMBER	2-3 hills	3-5'	No	4-5 per hill	No	4-6' between hills / 4-6' between rows	
EGGPLANT	2-3 plants	4-6'	3-4'	1	6	12" stagger planting	16"
PEPPERS	2-3 plants	4-6'	3-4'	1	6	12" stagger planting	16"
PUMPKINS	2-3 hills	12-18'	No	4-5 per hill	No	5-8' between hills / 6-10' between rows	

* These are plants started by sprinkling seeds in the row and then thinning by hand or by dragging a garden rake through the row. Peas and beans are easier to seed by hand and do not need thinning. The numbers per row are approximate for all small seeds. Remember, they do need room to grow.

YEAR_____

Average last frost date in spring:_____   Average first frost date in fall:_____

Varieties planted and "sure crop" recommendations	Date Planted	Date of First Harvest	Succession crop and date	Comments
Tenderpod; Tendergreen Improved			Try second crop of beans, beets, or carrots.	Pick young, before individual beans are visible in the pod.
Blue Lake; Kentucky Wonder; Romano			Try second crop of beans, beets, or carrots.	Pick young, before individual beans are visible in the pod.
Fordhook 242			No	Plant after ground warms up. Bear continuously all season.
			No	Plant 5-6 seeds per hill. Later thin to best 3-4 plants.
Early: Early Sunglow. Late: Butter and Sugar. Latest: Silver Queen			Plant seed at 2-week intervals to stretch harvest.	Pick immediately before serving to prevent natural sugars in the ear from turning to starch.
Slicing: Marketmore 76. Pickling: Wisconsin SMR18			No	Plant 5-6 seeds per hill. Later thin to best 3-4 plants.
Black Beauty			No	Transplants are a good idea in the North.
California Wonder			No	Transplants in the North. Likes poor soil. Leave green peppers on plant for red peppers.
Sweet Sugar; Jack-o'-Lantern			No	Needs space to sprawl. Grow as a barrier around corn to keep raccoons out.

NOTES:

YOUR CUSTOMIZED CHART FOR PLANNING AND PLANTING

Annual Vegetable	Amount to plant per person	Feet of row per person		Plants /ft. after thinning* or transplants/ft.		Distance between plants	Width of wide row
		Single row	Wide row	Single row	Wide row		
TENDER VEGETABLES *(continued)*				*(Plant on the average last frost date.)*			
SQUASH (zucchini and summer)	2-3 hills	5-10'	No	4-6 seeds in each hill	No	3-4' between hills 3-4' between rows	
SQUASH (winter)	2-3 hills	12-18'	No	4-6 seeds in each hill	No	5-8' between hills 6-10' between rows	
TOMATO	3-5 plants	10-15'	No		No	18-36"	
WATERMELON	3-5 hills	25-40'	No		No	5-8' between hills 6-10' between rows	
SOUTHERN FAVORITES							
COLLARDS	¼ pkt.	4-6'	3-4'	1*	5-6*	10-12" stagger planting	20"
MUSTARD GREENS	¼ pkt.	3-5'	1-3'	8-12*	24*	4-5"	16"
OKRA	2 plants	3-5'	No	1-2	No	10-12"	16"

* These are plants started by sprinkling seeds in the row and then thinning by hand or by dragging a garden rake through the row. Peas and beans are easier to seed by hand and do not need thinning. The numbers per row are approximate for all small seeds. Remember, they do need room to grow.

YEAR_____				
Average last frost date in spring:_____			**Average first frost date in fall:_____**	
Varieties planted _____ and "sure crop" recommendations	**Date Planted**	**Date of First Harvest**	**Succession crop and date**	**Comments**
Elite; Yellow: Early Straightneck			No	For extra-early crop, start some indoors and transplant.
Delicata; Acorn			No	Needs space to sprawl. Grow as a barrier around corn to keep raccoons out.
Roma for sauce; Pixie or Patio for small spaces; Big Boy; Better Boy			No	Start indoors. Transplant after danger of frost passes.
			No	Start indoors. Grow under plastic tunnels for head start in the North.
Georgia			Can follow early crop like lettuce.	A fall crop in the South. Flavor improves after light frost. Sometimes planted spring and fall.
Fordhook; Tendergreen			Can follow early crop like lettuce.	Often a fall crop in the South.
Spineless			No	Likes hot weather. Harvest when pods are 4" long or less.
NOTES:				

INDEX

Page numbers in italics indicate tables or illustrations.